MW01629996

Maud's Country

LANDSCAPES
that inspired the art of
MAUD LEWIS

Photographs
BOB BROOKS

Text
LANCE WOOLAVER

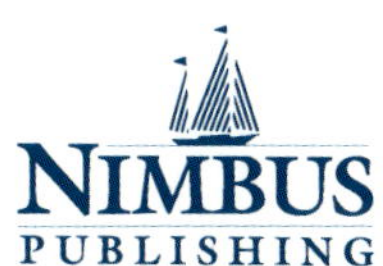

NIMBUS
PUBLISHING

Nimbus Publishing Limited
PO Box 9301, Station A
Halifax, NS   B3K 5N5
(902)455-4286

Design: Steven Slipp, Semaphor Design

Printed and bound in Hong Kong

Canadian Cataloguing in Publication Data

Woolaver, Lance, 1948–
Maud's country

ISBN 1-55109-314-6

1. Lewis, Maud, 1903–1970.   2. Painters—
Nova Scotia.   I. Brooks, Bob.   II. Title.

ND249.L447W664 1998   759.11
C98-950274-0

Nimbus Publishing acknowledges the financial
support of the Canada Council and the
Department of Canadian Heritage.

Acknowledgements

I wish to thank my daughter, Beth Brooks;
Jannet Kimber and Karen Ruggles of Carsand
Mosher, Halifax; and Steven Slipp of Semaphor
Design.

—B.B.

Maud Lewis paintings on pages 15, 22, 61
from the collection of Bob and Marion Brooks.
All other paintings are from the Woolaver
collection.

All photography of artwork by Bob Brooks
with the exception of pages 7 and 8.

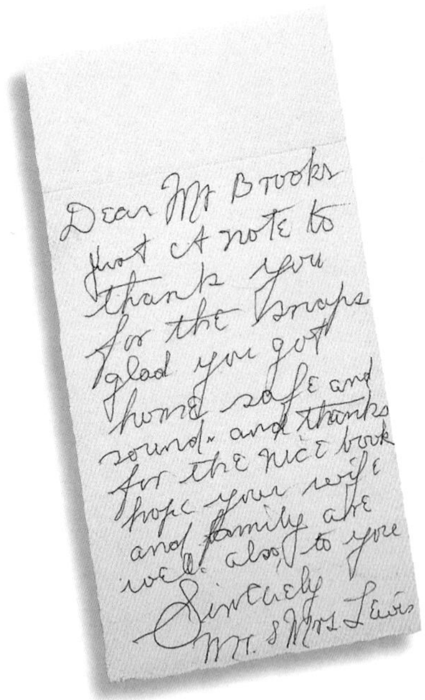

Foreword

✻ BOB BROOKS ✻

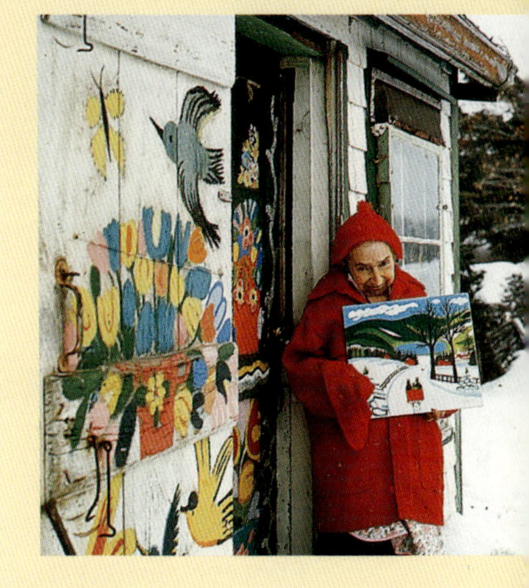

Maud poses outside her tiny house.

WHEN the Toronto *Star Weekly* contacted me in February 1965 to do a photo-story on the artist Maud Lewis, I had no idea who she was. But when they described her house in Digby County, and her bright, child-like paintings of oxen and cats, I knew immediately. I had passed the tiny doll-like house with the gaudily painted door and window countless times, and had seen the paintings for sale hanging outside. Although I knew nothing of its inhabitants, one couldn't help but notice the ten-by-twelve house—it was part of the local landscape.

Editors at the *Star Weekly* (a magazine that specialized in news and human interest stories) had seen a December episode of the popular CBC television program *Telescope* featuring a piece about this cheerful diminutive artist who lived with her husband in a little house in Marshalltown, Digby County, Nova Scotia. They thought that the quaint story would appeal to their readers.

At that time, Maud Lewis was a virtual unknown in the world of Canadian art. Folk art (and Maud Lewis) were more of a novelty than anything—indeed, when the *Star Weekly* article was published on July 10, 1965, it was titled "The Little Old Lady Who Painted Pretty Pictures," and referred to Lewis's art as "primitive painting." Today, some thirty-four years later, and after many more magazine articles, television, radio, and film documentaries, not to mention books, a play, and a national tour of her work, Maud Lewis is arguably Canada's best-known folk artist.

The photographs I took for the *Star Weekly* assignment were the result of a wintery day and evening spent with Maud and her husband. I had tried to phone the Lewises to arrange a shoot, but little did I know they had no phone, electricity, or even indoor plumbing. When I arrived at the house, which was so close to the main highway that it appeared to be in the ditch, a tall thin man with a toothless grin answered my knock on the door. After I introduced myself and stated my business, he stuck out a huge bear-like hand, and invited me into the miniature house. He was Everett Lewis—Maud's husband.

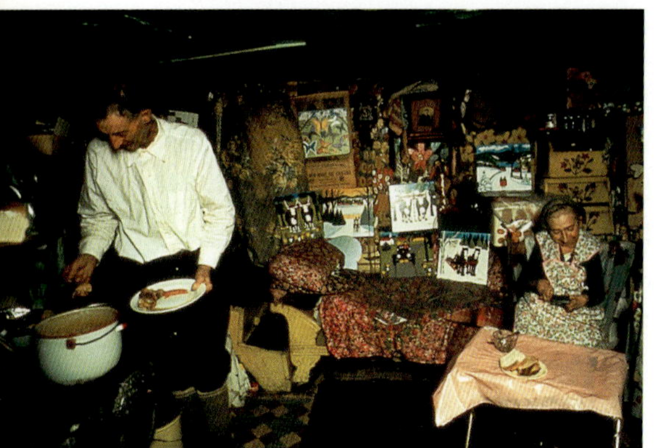

Everett serves up the evening meal to Maud.

Everett had been a local fish peddler and night watchman at a nearby poor farm, and had met Maud while he was selling fish door to door. They had been living in that house since their marriage, twenty-seven years before.

The house was essentially one room, with crude stairs leading to a loft that seemed to serve as their bedroom. The ceiling downstairs was covered with foil from cigarette packages, and was so low that Everett almost had to bend over when he stood up.

My first impression was of a cluttered darkness. As I got accustomed to the dim light, I turned toward a little voice that seemed to be coming from a gnome-like person hunched over a little TV table. This was my introduction to Maud Lewis. Surrounding this tiny person was a splash of jumbled colour, including bright paintings, cans of paint, and stacks of newspaper—all illuminated by a small window painted with brightly coloured tulips.

I said something amusing to break the ice, but Maud said, "I'm not dressed for pictures, and I'm a mess." She giggled behind her hand— something she did many times during the twelve hours I spent with her. Maud's eyes were sparkling, and full of mischief.

She was very interested in my equipment, and was amused with my antics—so much so that both Maud and Everett became comfortable with my presence and allowed me complete freedom. As a photographer, I try to act as a "fly on the wall"—if I'm successful, my subjects will go about their normal routine. In Maud Lewis's case, especially given the size of the house, I probably came as close as possible to capturing an average "day in the life of the Lewises."

During the shoot, Everett puttered around the tiny room, and mumbled back and forth with Maud. Maud painted for the entire day, often talking softly to her paintings. I got the sense that Everett was like a mother bird protecting its young. But my main concern was Maud and her art. Because of her tiny stature, she was huddled over her table, which prevented me from seeing her face, so I knelt in order to photograph her. There was such limited floor space I had to put one camera bag outside.

Maud seemed happy as she painted, and at times hummed. But for hours, she painted without a word. She used a Campbell's Soup can for her brushes, and old sardine tins for paints. I noticed that she did a painting completely, starting with the sky and working to the bottom edge. Because of her arthritis, Maud's fingers were gnarled, making her hands look like potatoes with fingers. She had to hold her brush between her first two fingers, and her brush strokes were more like dabs. It was remarkable how she managed. Maud never once complained, and seemed pleased to have a guest. Later in the day, she even asked my advice on using a particular

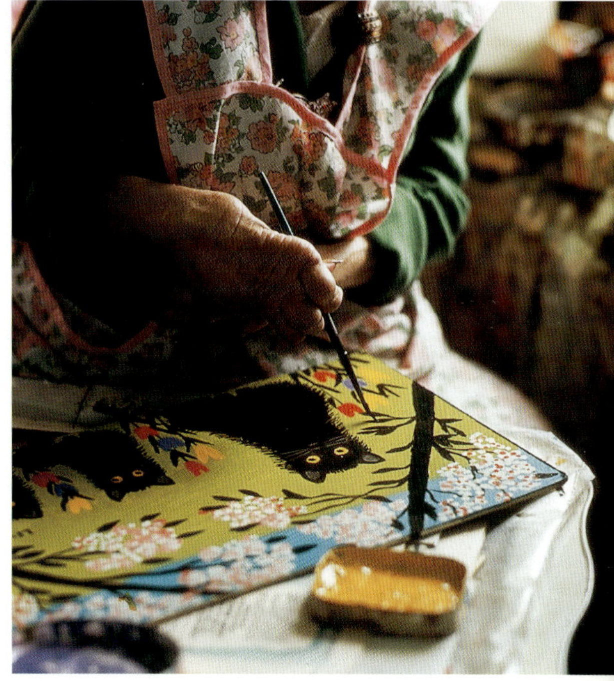

Maud puts the finishing touches to a painting.

colour. At one point, when I had to ask her to look up from her painting and smile, she did so laughing, with merry eyes.

All this time, Everett was restocking the woodbox inside for the stove. He also made tea, which we all shared. The rather tranquil scene of Maud painting and Everett puttering around was interrupted frequently by the noise of cars splashing chunks of snow against the tiny roadside house.

It took a lot to convince Maud Lewis that people wanted to see her, not just her paintings. I asked if she wouldn't mind helping me get a picture of her outside, holding one of her paintings. Everett helped Maud into a bright red coat, and she pulled on a matching red stocking-cap. She still had on her apron underneath, and wore her zipper slippers outside. She brought out a painting of winter sleighs, which she had just finished. The sleeves of her coat were so long that they acted like mittens when she posed for my camera. She was very shy and hid behind the twelve-by-four painting, but soon became accustomed to my amusing coaxing, and cooperated fully.

When we returned to the warmth of the little house, Maud handed Everett the painting of the sleighs and another of a Model T Ford to put in the warming oven above the stove in order to dry the paint. Everett helped her off with her coat, and she immediately went back to painting silently. Everett asked if I wanted to help him check his rabbit snares and take some "snaps" of him cutting up firewood. They had a rather primitive backyard, with a dog, bucksaw, and a few out-buildings. Everett had caught a rabbit, which he proceeded to skin.

As evening enveloped the tiny house, and the cars splashed by, I told them that I wanted to get a picture of them at dinner with their oil lamp. I wiped the steam off the small window and photographed the two of them having fresh rabbit stew, listening to the battery-powered radio. The Lewises appear to have cherished this picture, which was used by the *Star Weekly;* years later, during the restoration of their house, it was found taped to a cabinet door.

The *Star Weekly* article came out in July 1965, at which time I sent the Lewises prints of "my day with them." In return, I received a hand-painted thank-you note from Maud, with flowers painted on its cover flap—a truly thoughtful gesture. I went back to visit Maud and Everett a few times in later years, and they were always happy to see me.

Although I never really thought about it at the time, it seems that Maud painted images similar to those that attract a photographer: fishing villages, quaint coves, flowers, foliage, and people in every-day settings. The brighter the better. Maud, however, had the advantage of artistic license, and painted whatever combination of place and subject she fancied. Photographers, apart from using digital manipulation, have to take pretty much what they get through the lens of the camera. I have taken pictures throughout Nova Scotia of fishing villages, the sea, landscapes, farmers, little white churches, and fields of flowers. While the scenes that Maud painted might not have been the spitting image of the real thing, for the most part, the details of sea and landscapes do—or did—exist in the country that surrounded her in Nova Scotia.

Introduction

✻ LANCE WOOLAVER ✻

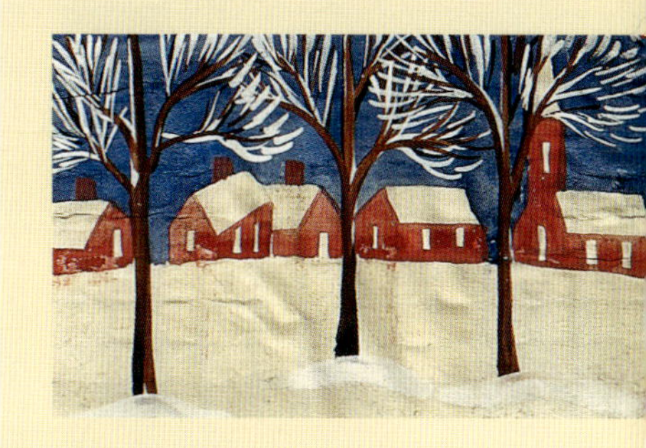

VERY YEAR brings some happiness and every year brings some sadness, but it is rare for one to bear extremes of both.

In June 1997, I was in Yarmouth, Nova Scotia. I had paid to have a stone placed on the grave of Maud Lewis's mother, Agnes Dowley, who had been buried in an unmarked grave sixty-two years before—a practice once spoken of as being "buried on the town." Earlier that year, in examining some old "Maud Lewis" Christmas cards, I was pleased to find the name "A. Dowley" inscribed on the back, leading me to believe the old story that Maud had been taught to paint by her mother. This discovery was a great joy to me, imagining Maud and her mother painting Christmas cards together; however, I couldn't bear the thought of the unmarked grave. Maud's work had witnessed a great revival, and I asked myself what Maud would have wanted from this success— hence the stone.

During my first visit to the cemetery, I knocked on the door of the custodian, who turned out to be an old classmate. "Her brothers are here, too," he said. That was when I learned that Maud had had two brothers, Victor and George, who had died in infancy. They had been buried in the common grave. From the records we were able to ascertain their ages, which we added to the stone.

The day of the dedication was grey and threatened rain. I had invited friends and relatives of the Dowleys whom I knew. The service started happily and the rain held off. Then, it came my turn to speak. I was unable to hold back tears, and gasped the few lines I had prepared for the occasion. After years of researching and writing about Maud Lewis's life, from her youth in Yarmouth to her married life in the neighbouring county of Digby, I realized there was still much to do to honour her gift to the world.

Maud Lewis became a celebrity nearly thirty years after her death. Today she is popularly referred to in the press as "Canada's best-loved folk artist," and somewhat inaccurately as "Canada's Grandma

Moses." This posthumous fame stands in stark contrast to her daily life. She was born near the port town of Yarmouth on the southwest tip of Nova Scotia in 1903, and lived there with her parents until their passing in the 1930s. She painted Christmas cards with her mother to augment the family income. In 1934, she moved to Digby to live with an aunt, but soon after she married Everett Lewis, a fish peddler and night watchman at the county poor farm next door. For the rest of her life, Maud shared his ten-by-twelve-foot home beside the main road in Marshalltown, a few kilometres from Digby. Winter and summer she passed her time painting her now-familiar works, which she sold to passers-by for a few dollars. Her bright, cheerful legacy, created without fanfare, is growing with every passing year, as we capture her life and work in books, film, and theatre.

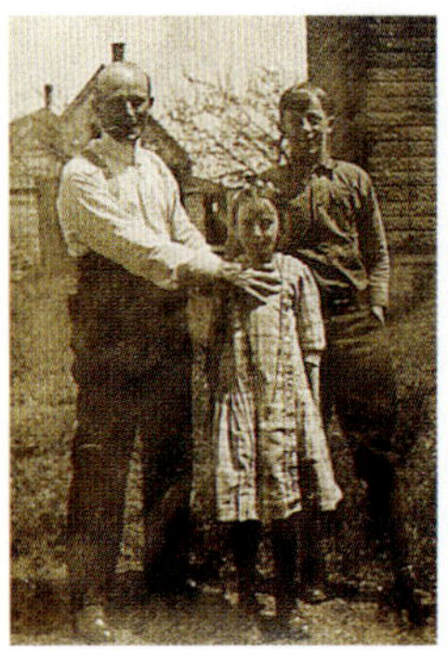 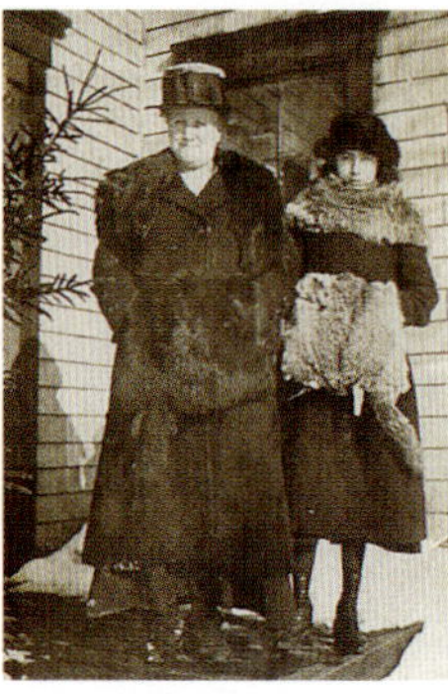

Left: Eight-year-old Maud, with father and brother Charles.

Right: Maud and Agnes Dowley.

After the dedication of the stone to Agnes Dowley and her two infant sons, I retraced Maud's journey from Yarmouth to Digby, to return to my own home, as I had done many times in the past few years. I drove up the dirt road to North Range, where Maud is buried with her husband's family. Her grave stands in the extreme north corner of this cemetery, and her maiden name, Dowley, is recorded on the stone. No one knows why Everett chose that inscription instead of Maud Lewis. There is no question about their being married and Maud proudly signed her letters "Mrs. Lewis."

This book presents the Nova Scotia that Maud Lewis loved—the towns, country roads, and farmyards. It shows her clear and innocent view of nature, and her love of rural living. It also features the work of photographer Bob Brooks, whose long association with Maud has made it possible to preserve her legacy.

There is very little left of Maud Lewis in the town where she was born and in the county where she lived. Her little house is now an "artifact" and has been removed. Her paintings are found all over North America. When we look at them, we see Nova Scotia as Maud knew it.

Maud's Country

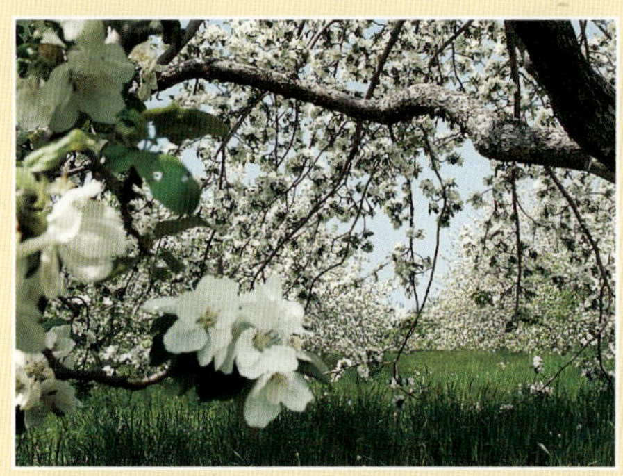

LANDSCAPES
that inspired the art of
MAUD LEWIS

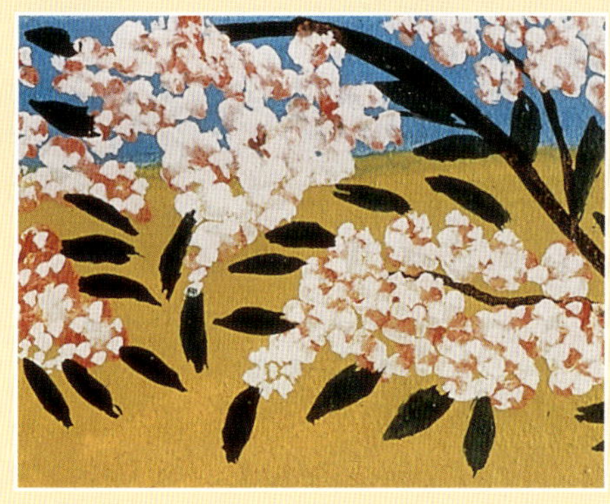

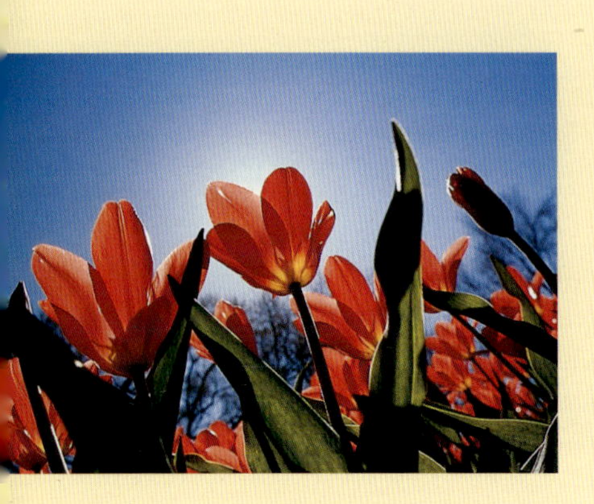

A FEW MILES DOWN THE ROAD from where Maud and Everett Lewis's house once stood is the studio of their friend, folk artist Stephen Outhouse. His carving of Ev is made from a tree that Ev himself planted in the 1940s. When the house was removed from the site and the property bulldozed for the parking lot for the Maud Lewis memorial, Outhouse took the tree and set to work.

He also took something else. Back in the bushes where Maud had enjoyed a little flower garden, Stephen found some daffodils that had endured both time and neglect. He dug them up and planted them on his own property, and they bloom every spring—a bequest from Maud to the world from which she drew her inspiration.

The house stood on low ground between the highway and the Poor Farm. On one side was a shallow well and to the rear a small pond that Ev had dug, fed by a passing brook. In addition to bringing daffodils, tulips and crocuses, spring also brought floods. The run-off from the road and the overflow from the brook often left the house more than a little damp. In the 1950s a solution to the problem was effected by moving the house back from the road onto a foundation.

Maud loved flowers and blossoms, so much so that she would paint them irrespective of other seasonal details. She is also famous for her paintings of oxen and cats. She painted more than two hundred of her most popular motifs for paid commissions, especially the teamed oxen under a spruce bough, and the black cats under spring blossoms. Left to her own devices, and granted an hour or two of respite from the arthritis that plagued her in later years, Maud painted flowers, especially the all-time spring favourites—daffodils and tulips. She was also very free with colours, not limiting herself to yellow daffodils and red tulips, but using colours she had on hand—mauve, pink, deep blue and even black—she gave her flowers a certain spontaneity.

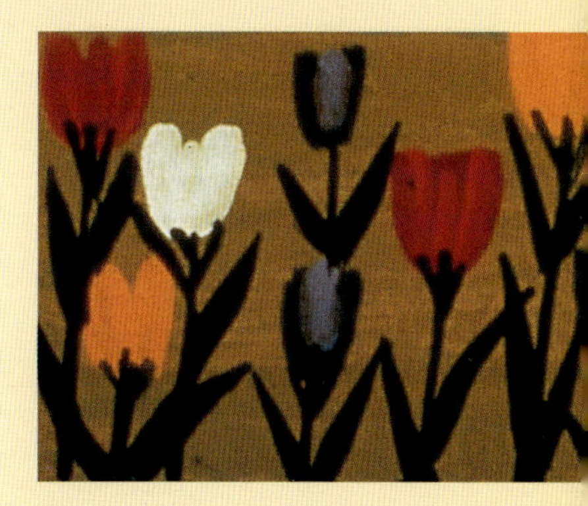

Among the most prolific of the wildflowers found in Nova Scotia are irises and wild orchids. Day lilies and Canada lilies are nearly wild, as they have survived, like Maud's daffodils, on old abandoned homesteads. Truly wild are blue flag and yellow flag irises, found beside streams, ditches and bogs all over the province. The most common wild orchid is the Lady Slipper, a delicate pink flower that is losing ground due to predation and invasion of the woodlands. One of Maud's favourite flowers was the escapee from lost gardens, Lily of the Valley. My father, Phillip Woolaver, transplanted the white variety to Maud's backyard.

Maud's paintings celebrate the persistence and determination of the natural world to shake off winter and burst into spring.

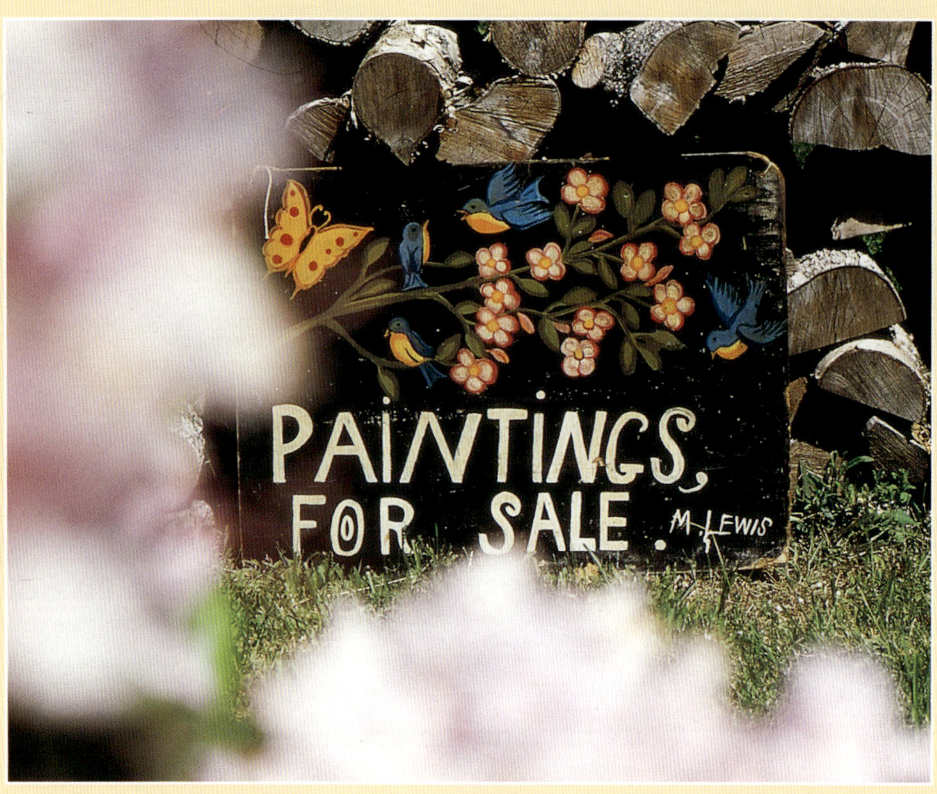

*This last two weeks we have had pretty good
weather, but it's rather cool at night. We have just
got our garden in. Seems to me every spring it gets
later for planting ... this Sunday is Apple Blossom
Sunday. If it's fine lots of cars will be coming by here.
We went trouting last Sunday and was gone all afternoon and only got two. The woods is awful pretty
now, the leaves are all out once again isn't it hard to
get things around here. I sent to Eaton's for
a house dress.*

Maud Lewis, Letter, Marshalltown, NS, May 30, 1947

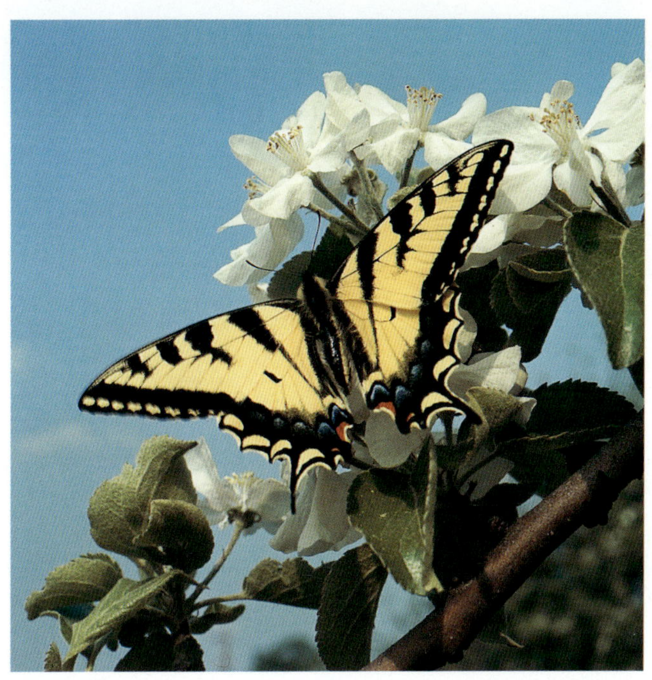

Well, we are getting a few fine days over here. But today it is all clouded up again ready for a rain. We had a hard time putting our garden in this year it's been such a cold Spring. Everything is going to be late growing. Carrots and things are just coming up though. ... news is scarce around here ... I can put scenery or butterflies on them what colour do you wish me to paint on them first, all black or some other. Snow scenery would show up good on a black background, better than a light shade.

Maud Lewis, Letter, Marshalltown, NS, June 19, 1945

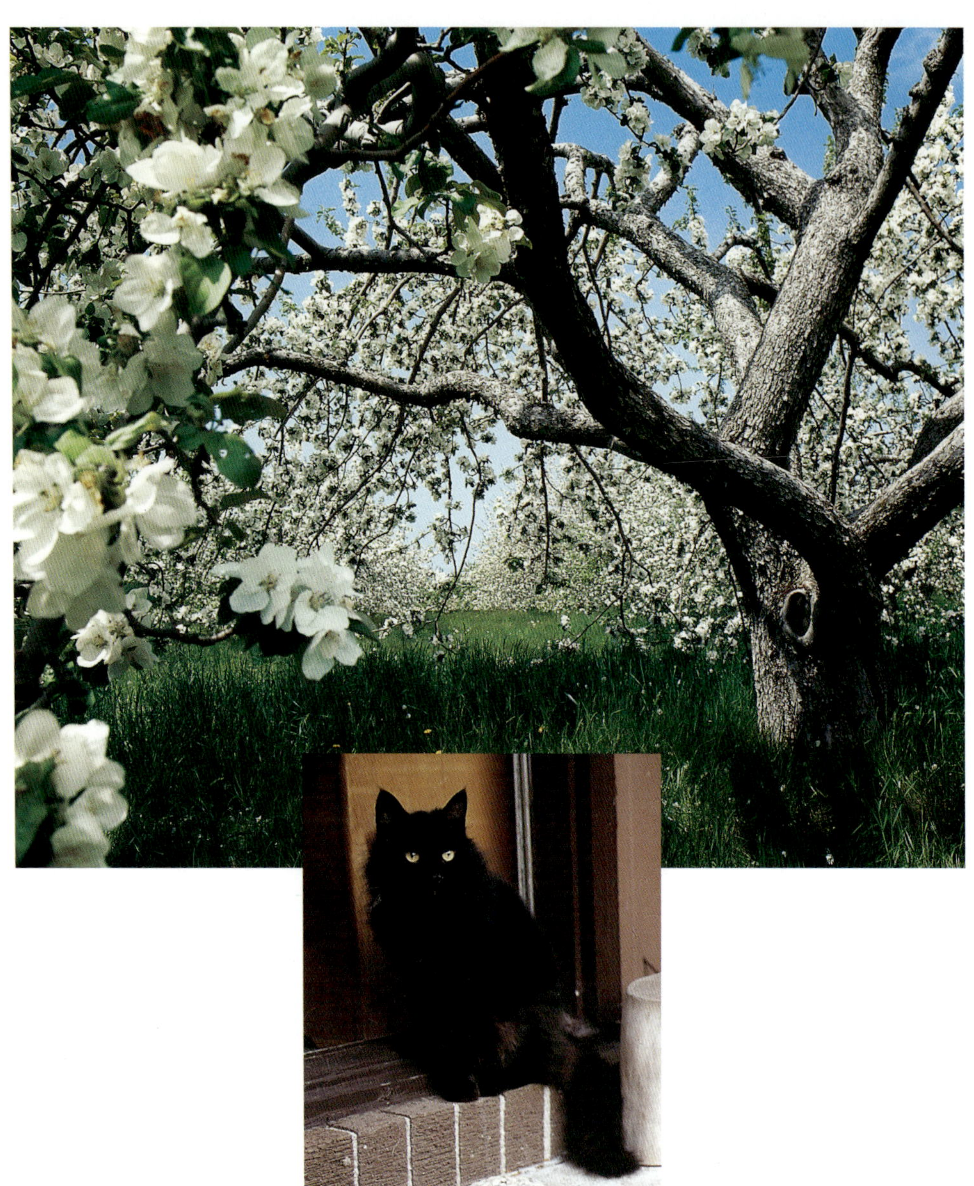

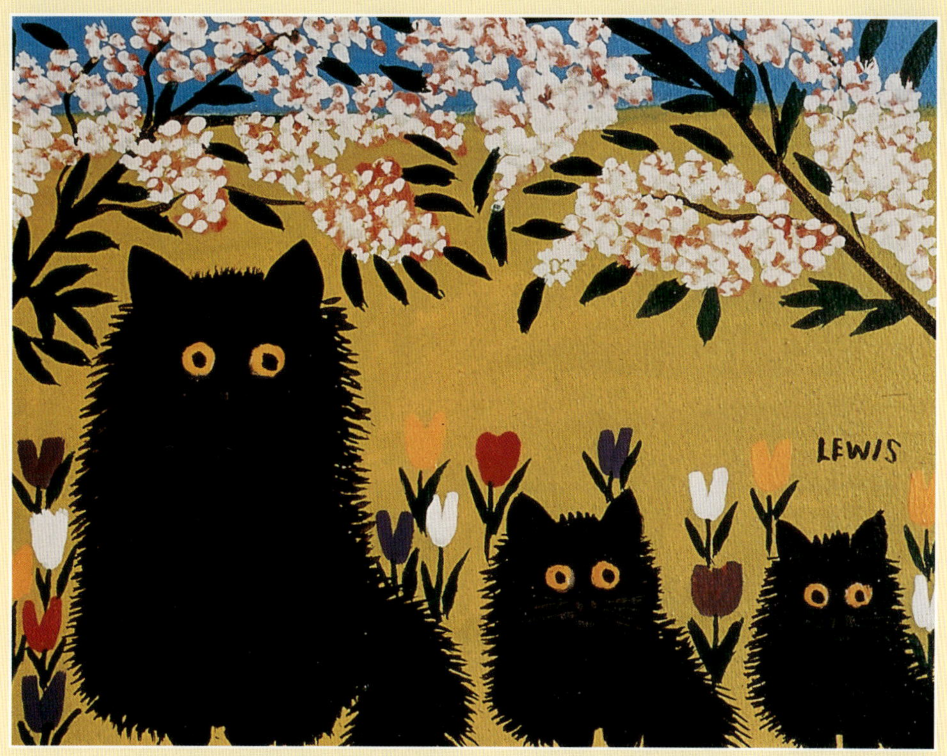

*Doug was there one day and Maud had this letter on her TV table.
There were little dabs of paint over it. And Doug asked what that
was, and she just handed him the letter. And he opened it up
and he looked at it. Doug said, "Are you going to send the White
House a painting?" And Everett said, "When they send their
money, we'll send a painting." The White House was of no
importance to Everett.*

Floss Lewis, Interview, Digby, NS, 1997

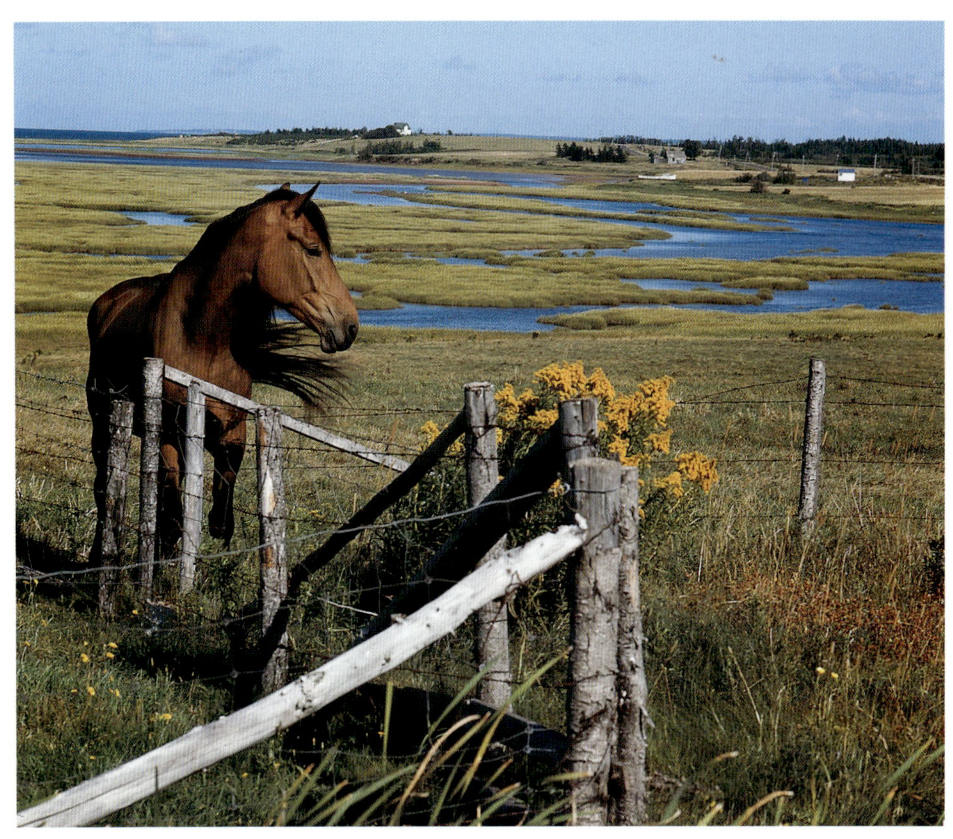

*Just a note to thank you for the snaps ... glad you got home safe
and sound and thanks for the nice book ... hope your wife
and family are well also to you.*

Maud Lewis, Letter to Bob Brooks, Marshalltown, NS, 1965

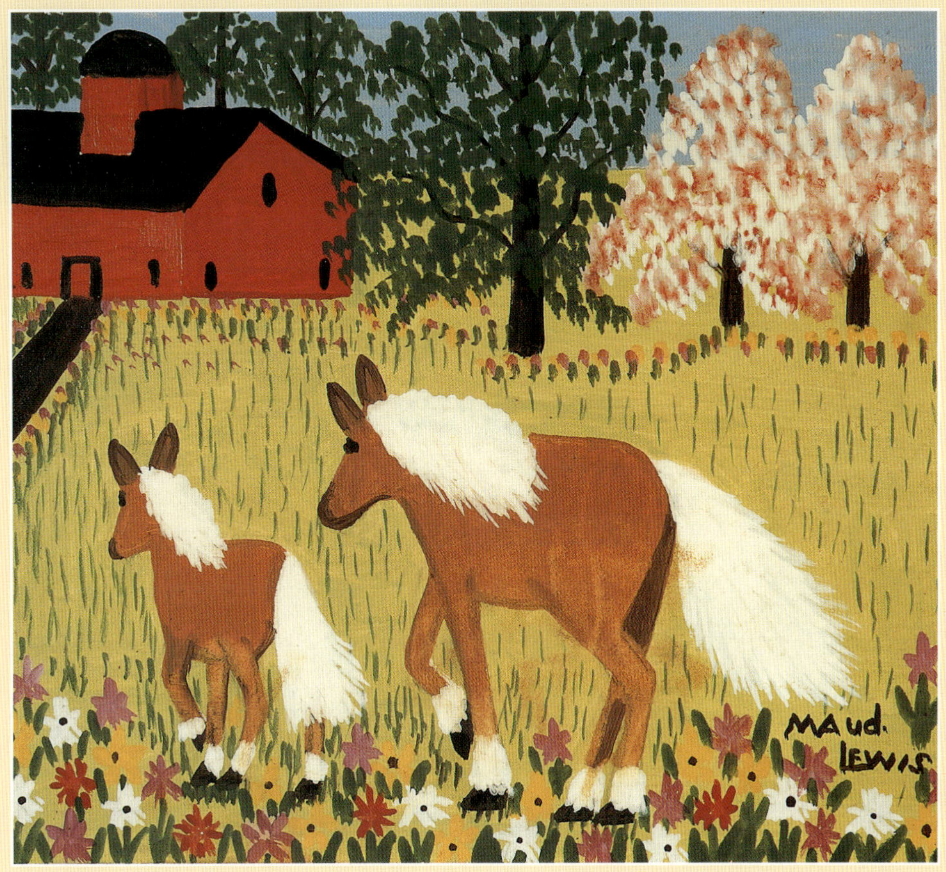

... In those early days, you know, when her paintings brought two dollars, three dollars, four dollars, it didn't look as though she had a bright future. But today the paintings are prized.

Nate Bain, Interview, Yarmouth, NS, 1997

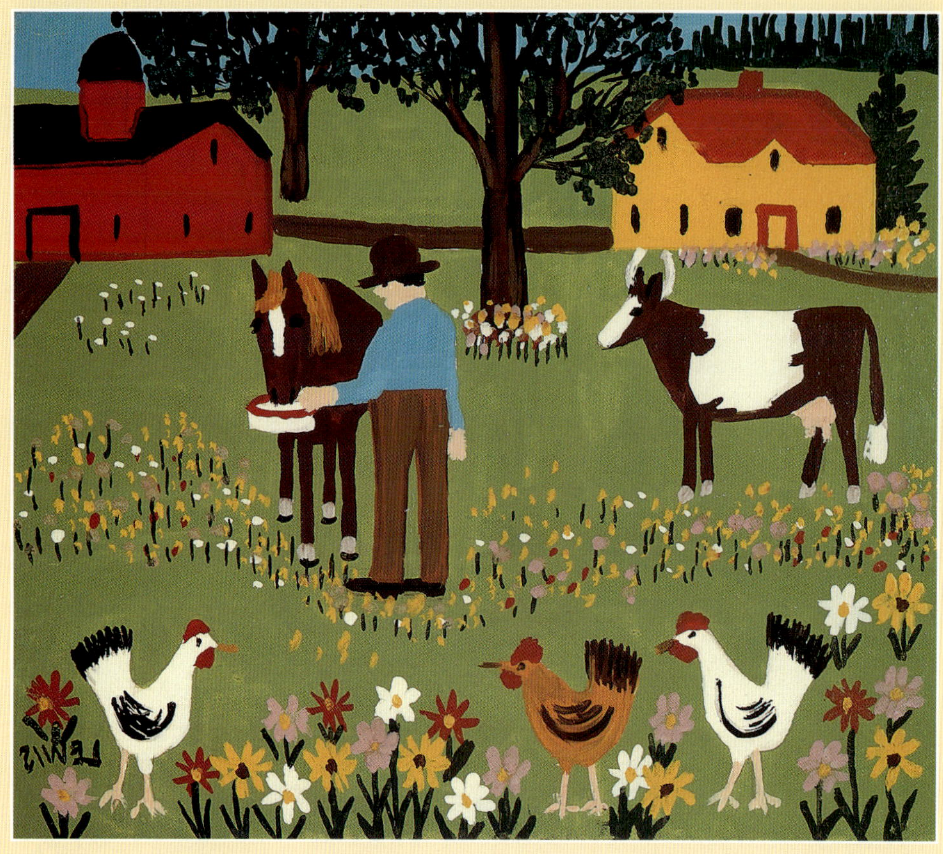

These are Maud's early works, fairly small works. They are much more detailed, busier, and she's taken much more time with the work. Little bit of humour here in the painting, I think, between the horse and the man and the chickens. I also like the way that she has the summer and the fall scene built into the painting with the red leaves, and the yellow and the green …
I love the sort of huge chickens.

Allan Deacon, Interview, Wolfville, NS, 1997

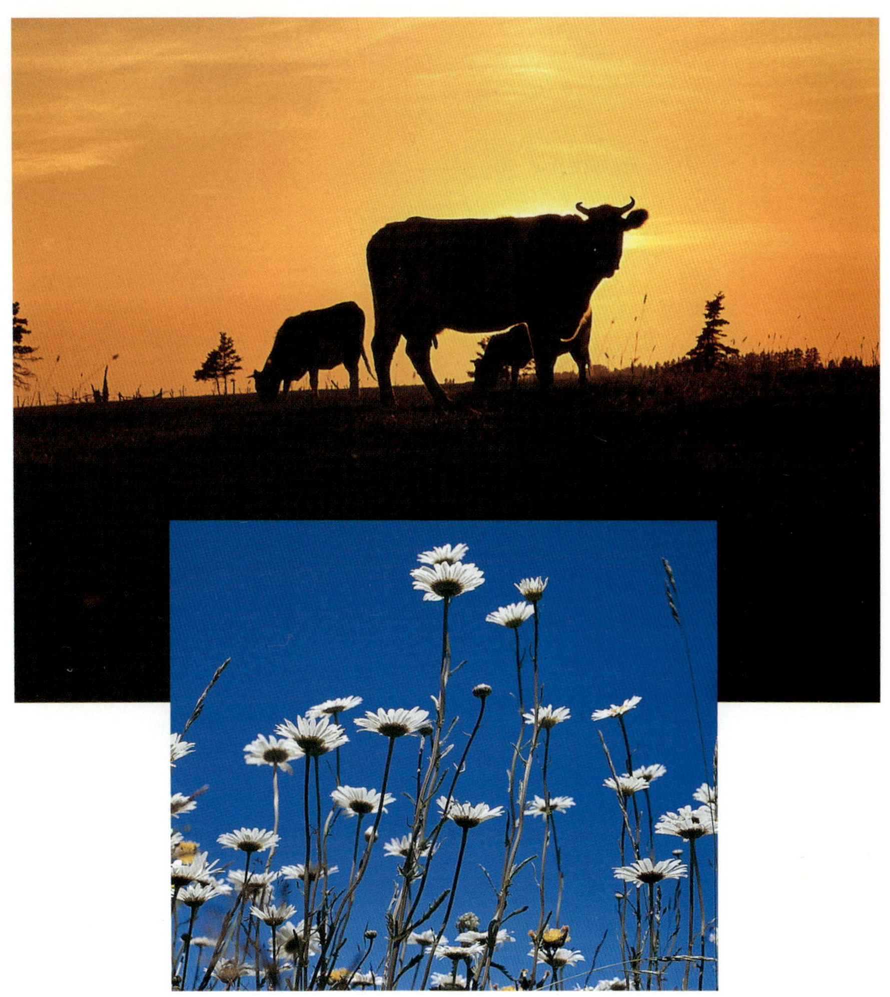

We first visited Maud at her little home near the No. 1 Highway at Marshalltown in the summer of 1966. Everett invited us into the house where Maud sat at the front window with her paints and canvasses surrounding her and working on a TV tray as a table. My parents and I wanted to purchase pictures, but she would only let us have one each, as she said other people would probably stop by and she wanted to save some for everyone. She reached down beside her chair and handed us each a picture. When we found out they were not signed, we asked her to autograph them. She was a bit reluctant ... but we insisted and she shyly signed them.

Mrs. Carol Hill, Letter, 1994

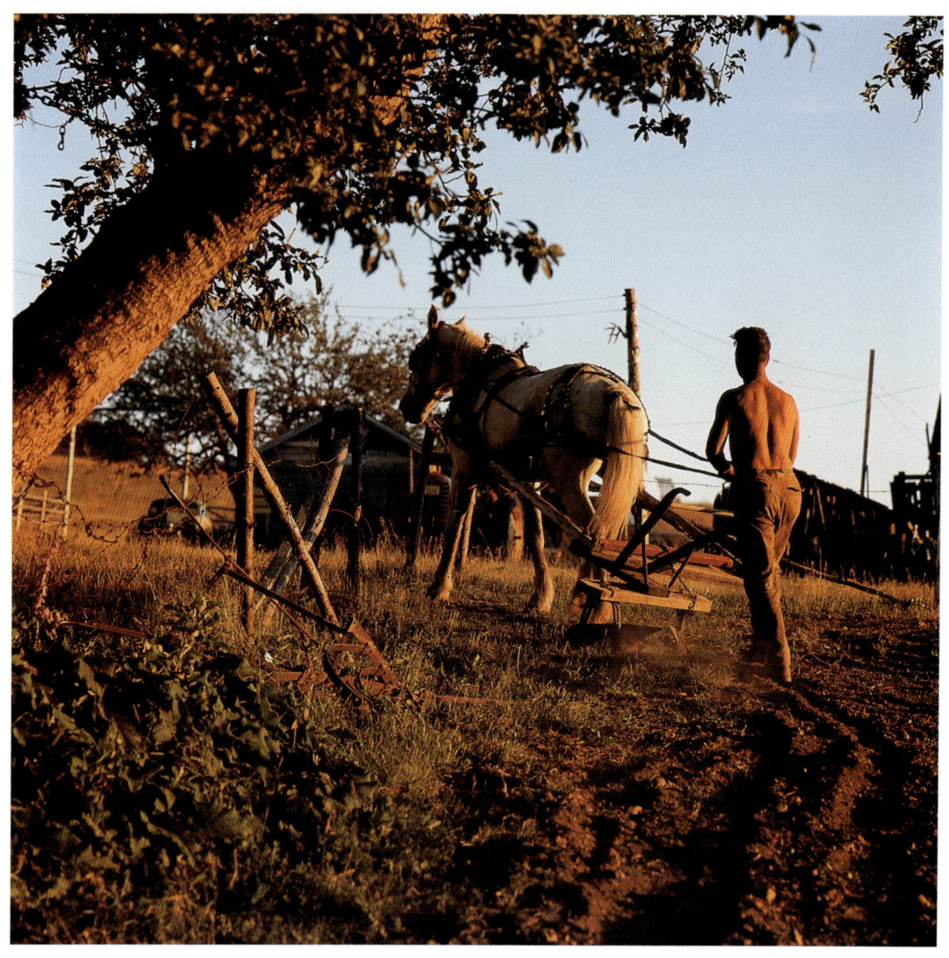

Everett worked for Mr. MacNeil had a farm up on the Ridge. Did a little of everything, plowing, chopped wood. Whatever he had for him to do. Before that he worked for Dr. Dickie. It was Dr. Dickie got him out of the Poor Farm.

Free Sibley, Interview, Marshalltown, Digby County, NS, 1995

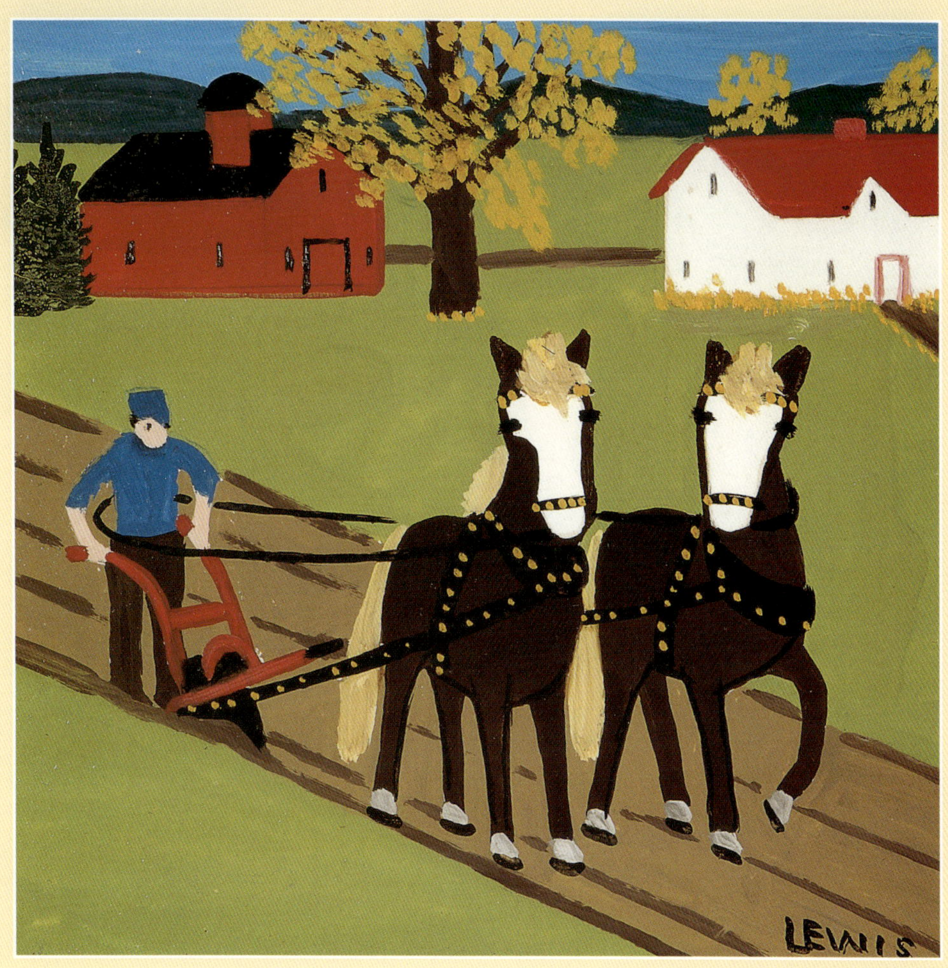

*Our people in Digby who were best off were farmers who worked
from first light till long after dark and managed to eke out enough
to eat and they clothed themselves beautifully from
the T. Eaton catalogue.*

Phillip Woolaver, Interview, Bear River, NS, 1997

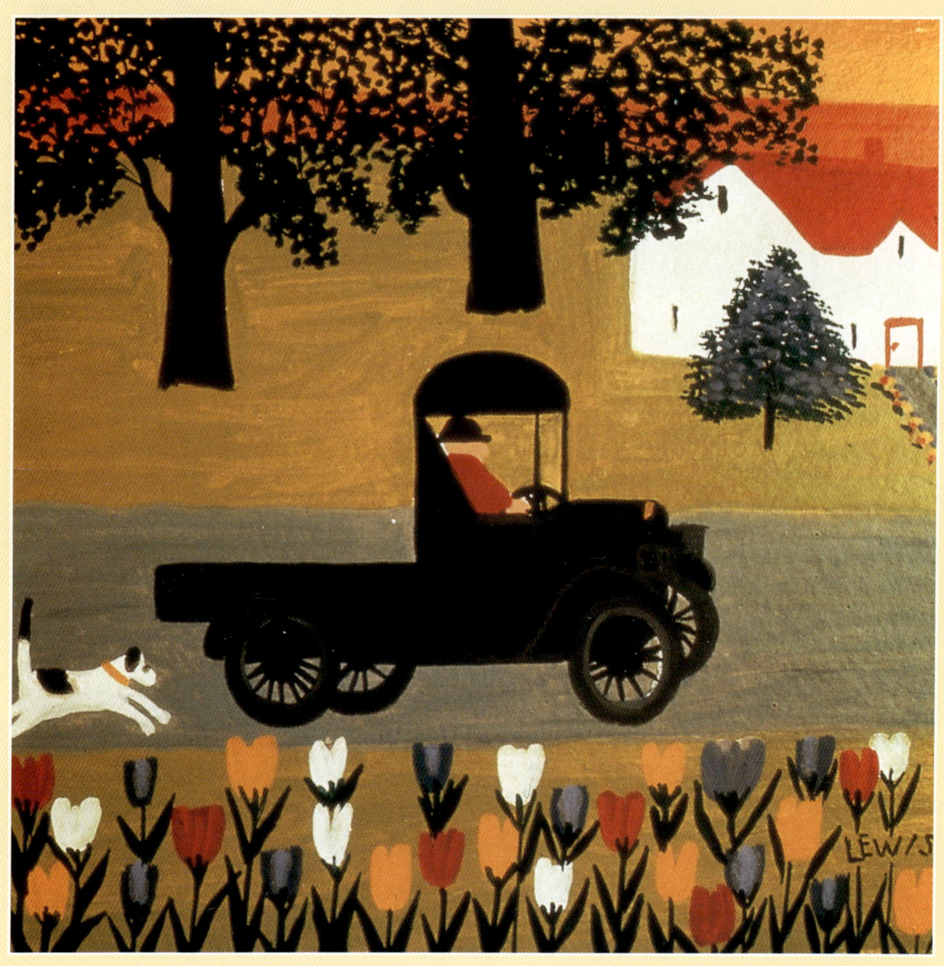

*I kept a dog then, a pretty sharp dog, wouldn't let anyone into
the house, but when Maud come he never said a word.
Now wasn't that funny?*

Everett Lewis, Interview, Marshalltown, NS, 1974

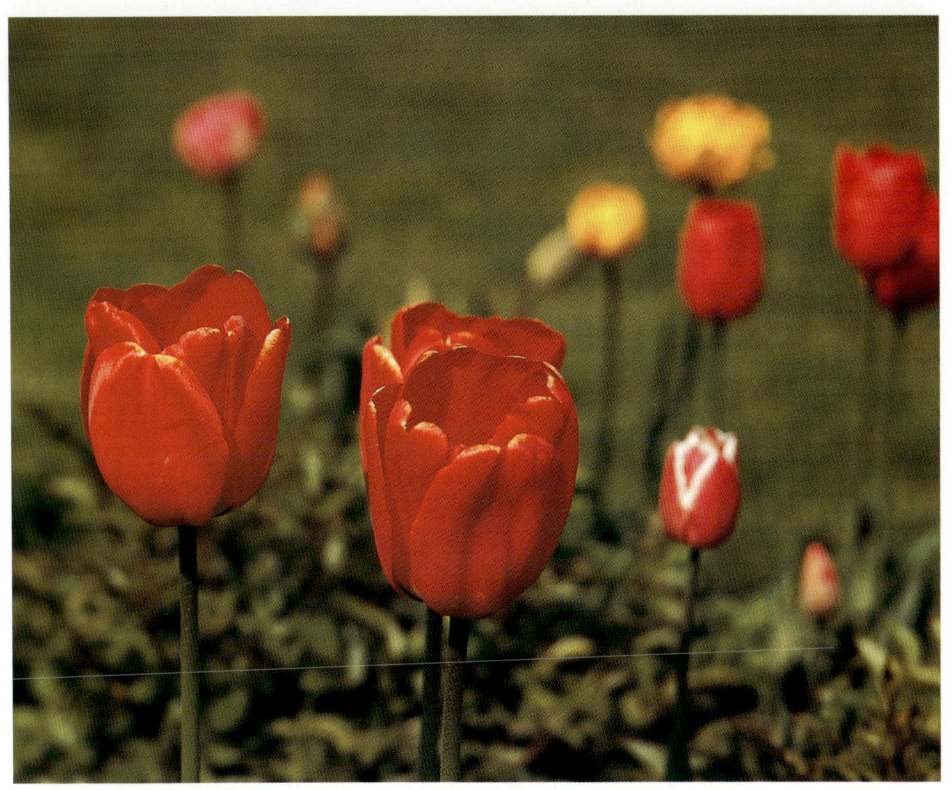

*There's always flowers in her paintings. So she really appreciated
gardens and flowers. She painted them even in her snow scenes,
she had tulips coming up here and there. I think she was just a
happy person and as long as she had paints and boards to paint
on she was perfectly happy.*

Floss Lewis, Interview, Digby, NS, 1997

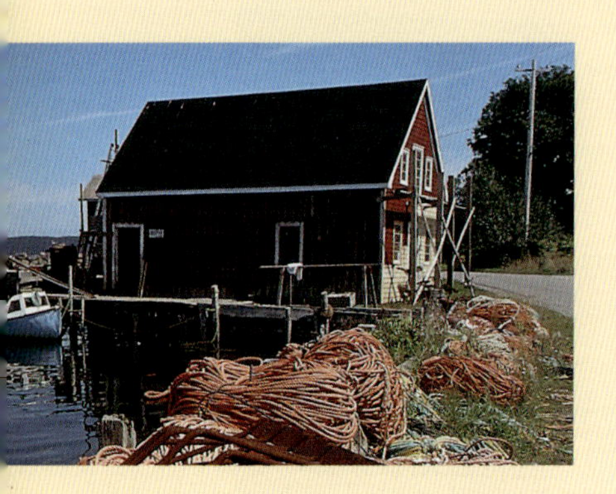

HAVING A ROADSIDE trade was not unusual. The Lewis's neighbours, the Amiraults, sold strawberries in season and Bert Potter, just down the road in Plympton, sold handmade quilts. Everett set Maud up by the highway—as her own advertisement. However, when the mosquitoes and flies became more active, she retreated inside and passers-by saw the sign as an invitation to stop for a chat and purchase a painting, usually only one per customer, especially in the busy season of summer.

Maud kept the paintings stacked near her, each one separated by matchsticks, which made small impressions in the wet paint, still visible today on many Maud Lewis originals. Tourists from Maine or New Brunswick, Airstream trailers from Ontario, and the famous Tauck Tour buses from New York, all came past Maud's house.

The measure of a true artist is that their work is a constant invitation to see the world through their eyes. It seems that many people were delighted to take home a piece of Maud's country, to see the world as she saw it, to supplement, no doubt, the landscapes that they had snapped with cameras, and the ones they held in their memories.

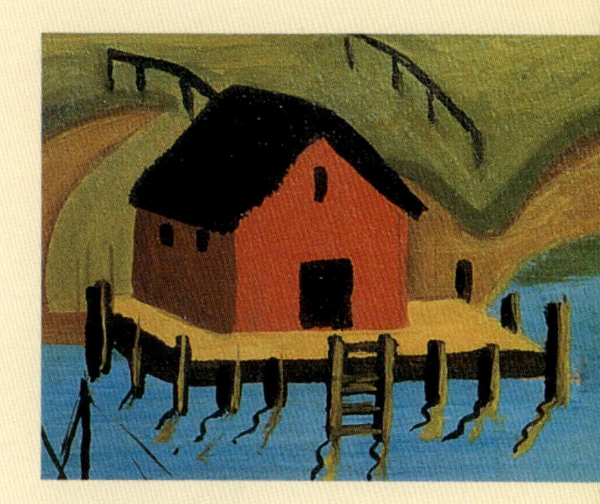

Her summer paintings are more leisurely than her winter ones. The boats are at anchor, or gently sailing by, the seagull is resting on one leg, the teamster and oxen are on their way home. Like a composer working with melody, Maud used colour in her own distinctive style. Summer was a time when she could really bring out the full range of her palette, with bluer skies and water, and greener fields and woods.

Summer also brought many friends to her door. They too wanted to buy paintings, and stay for chat. By the end of her life she was busy filling commissions from home and away. Sitting in her house, with the door open to refresh the air from the paint fumes, Maud Lewis would work away on the boards Ev cut for her. The summer outside was never as bright, however, as the summer of Maud's imagination.

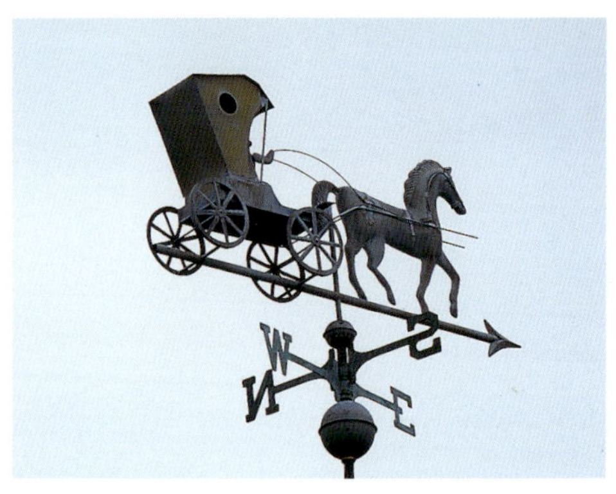

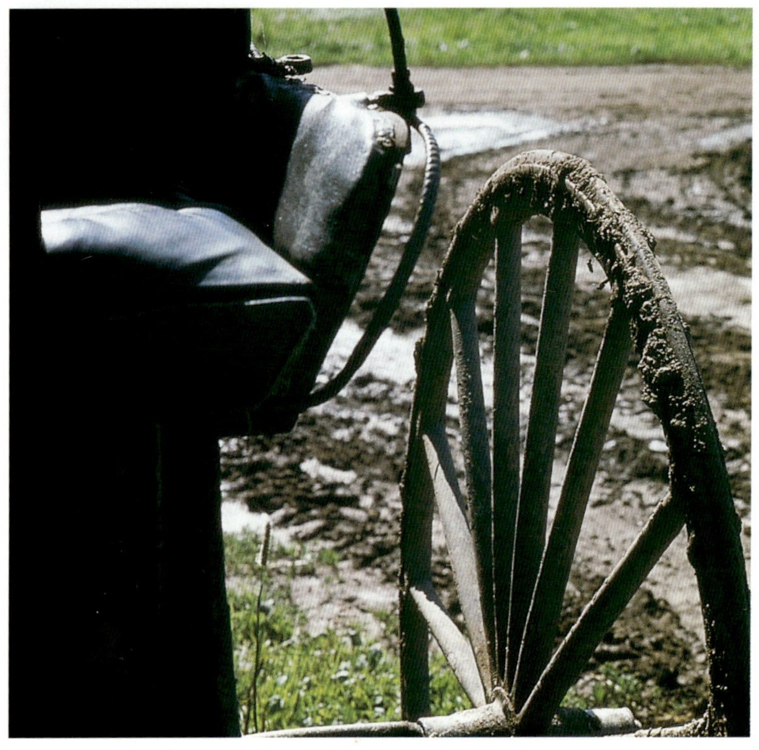

Father used to hire a horse and buggy and we'd be gone all day,
a span of horses, beach picnics, the whole family.
They're all dead now.

Maud Lewis, Interview, CBC *Telescope*, Marshalltown, NS, 1965

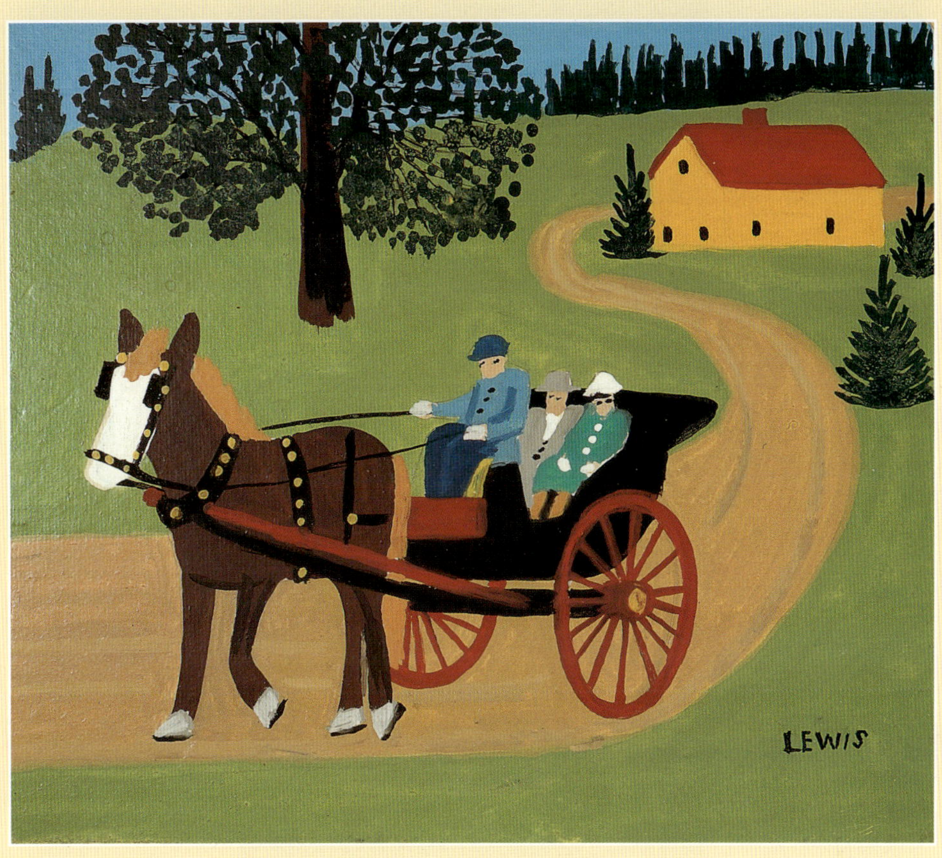

I mostly make up the ideas for the pictures myself, Mrs. Lewis said. She had only a couple of lessons in her girlhood when she was Maud Dowley of Yarmouth. These aroused her interest and in years since her late teens, she says, she has turned out a vast num- ber of paintings, how many she does not attempt to estimate.

Bert Wetmore, *Halifax Herald,* November 23, 1950

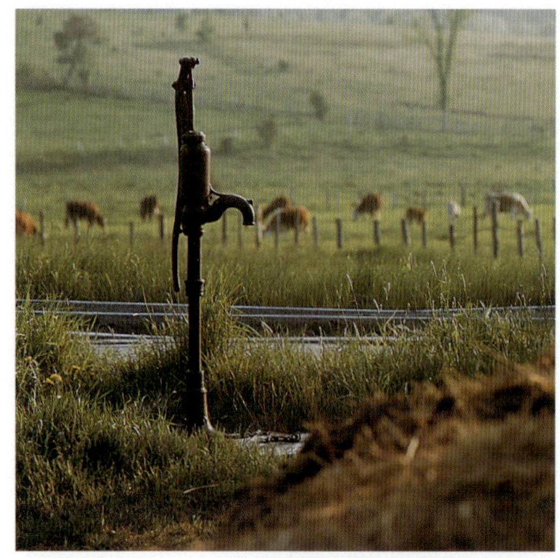

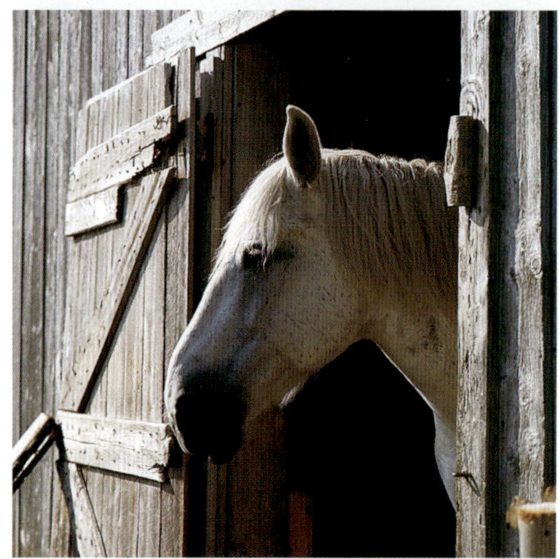

When I finally got inside, Mrs. Lewis greeted me shyly from the kitchen table. Because of her infirmity she sat with her head drooped forward and gazed at me with pretty, penetrating blue eyes. She answered my questions almost reluctantly and certainly with indifference. There were three and I chose one. She said, that would be seven dollars. As I studied her face, it was like looking at the expression of a sweet child, completely trusting and unsophisticated. Her gaze told me she was studying me too. Maybe I've turned up in one of her works as a horse or a happy dog.

Doris McCoy, Letter, Sarnia, Ontario, 1996

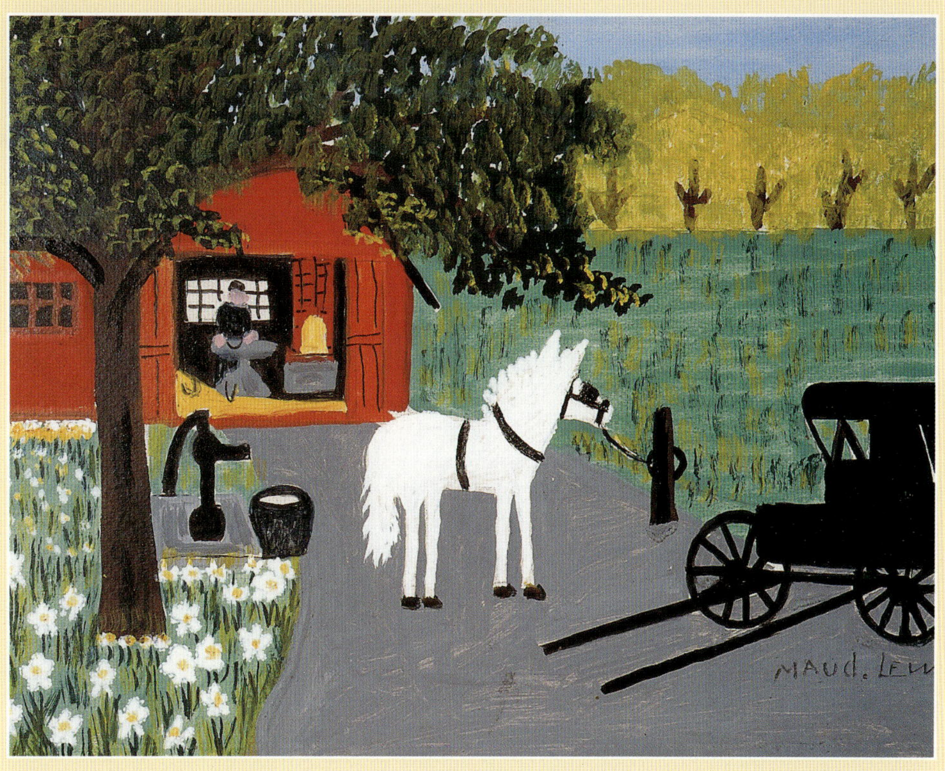

*And then I went along in the spring of 1969 and she had about ten
paintings and they were all stacked with slats of wood in between,
so very often you can pick up a Maud Lewis painting and you can
juggle it around and look for these sort of slat lines in the way
she dried the work. And she said to me, you can have any painting
you like. And I said, I'd like this one: it was a scene of a blacksmith
with a white horse. When I said, I'd like this one, she said,
I'm sorry, you can't have that one, it's for the doctor,
so I ended up taking another one.*

Allan Deacon, Wolfville, NS, 1997

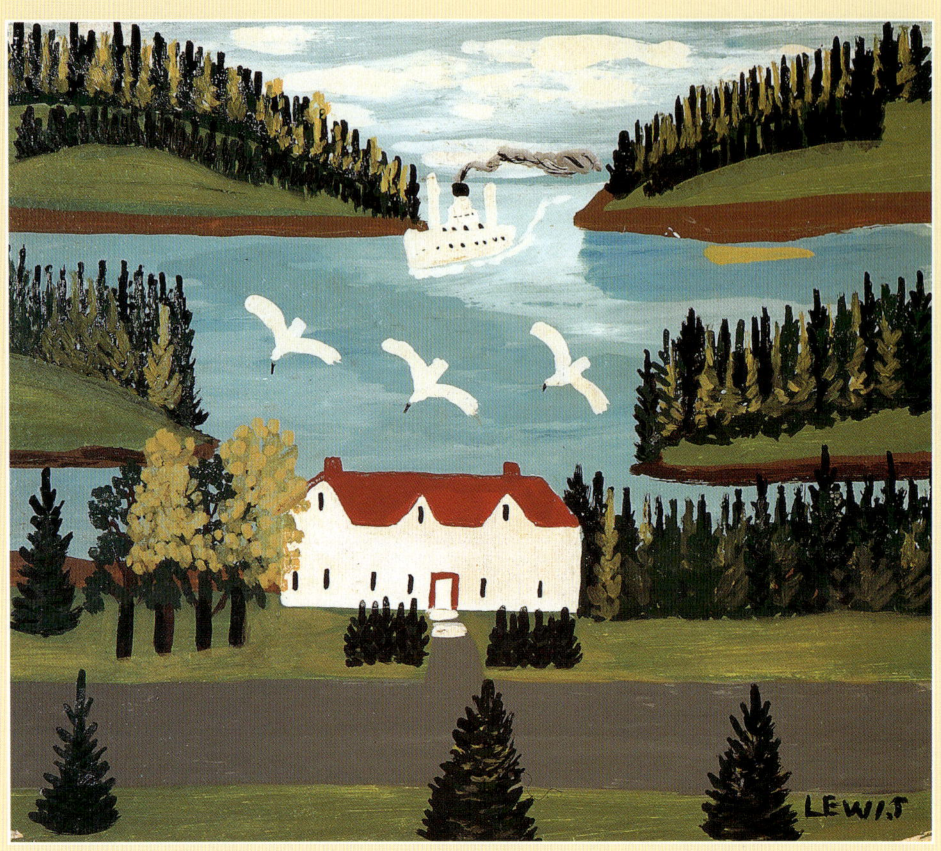

*The scenery of Digby County is both varied and picturesque.
Diversified by mountain, valley, lake and river, no part of the
Province or Dominion presents a more inviting field for the Tourist
and Pleasure Seeker.*

** * **

*Annapolis Basin, outlet of the River of that name, is a beautiful,
placid sheet of water, extending from the mouth of Bear River to
the remarkable strait called by the Aborigines "Tee-wee-den,"
signifying "Little Hole," or, by the English, "St. George's Channel,"
but now known as Annapolis and Digby Gut.*

Isaiah Wilson, *History of the County of Digby*, 1893

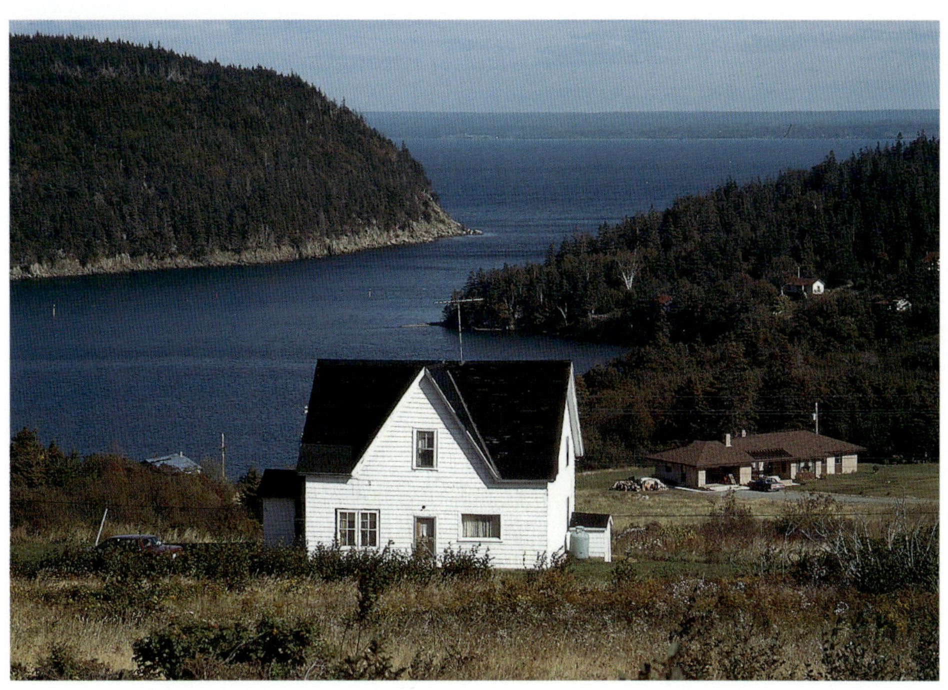

*Maud has lived all her life within the sixty miles of small farms,
fishing villages and lumber camps separating the towns of Digby
and Yarmouth on the southern tip of Nova Scotia, and only once
has been as far away as Halifax. But when Everett bought a
vintage Model T and took Maud peddling fish three days a week,
her vision of the farmyards and fishing boats took on the
magic of her happiness.*

Murray Barnard, *Star Weekly,* July 10, 1965

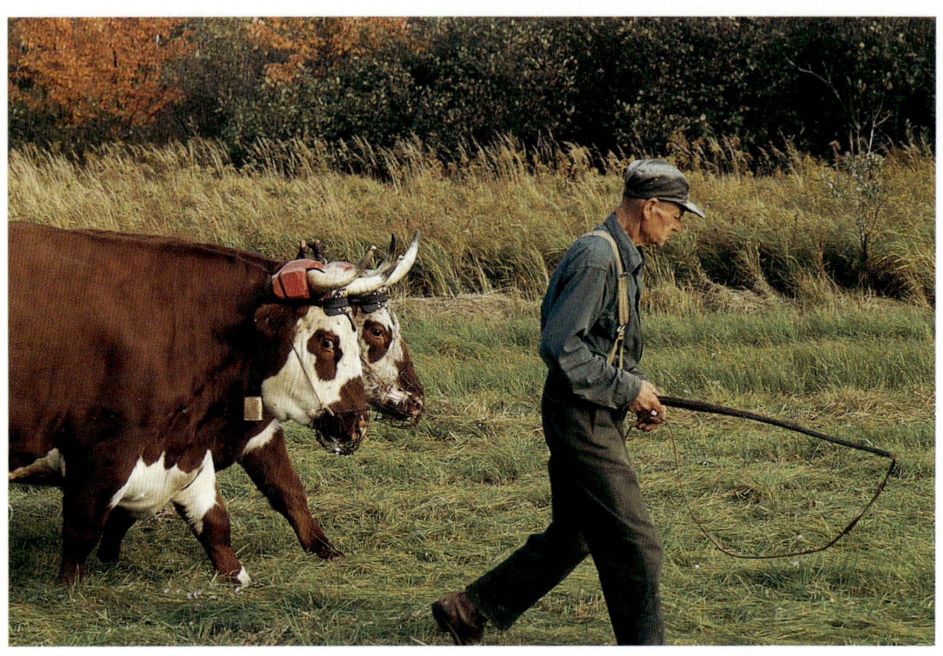

*Mrs. Maud Lewis is a tiny woman with large, twinkling blue eyes
that seem to see everything at once ... in spite of her infirmity she
has been painting steadily since she was eighteen years old.
She loves animals. She loves people. She loves life. Money, beyond
what is required to buy food and fuel, is a matter of complete
indifference to her.*

Doris McCoy, *Atlantic Advocate*, January 1967

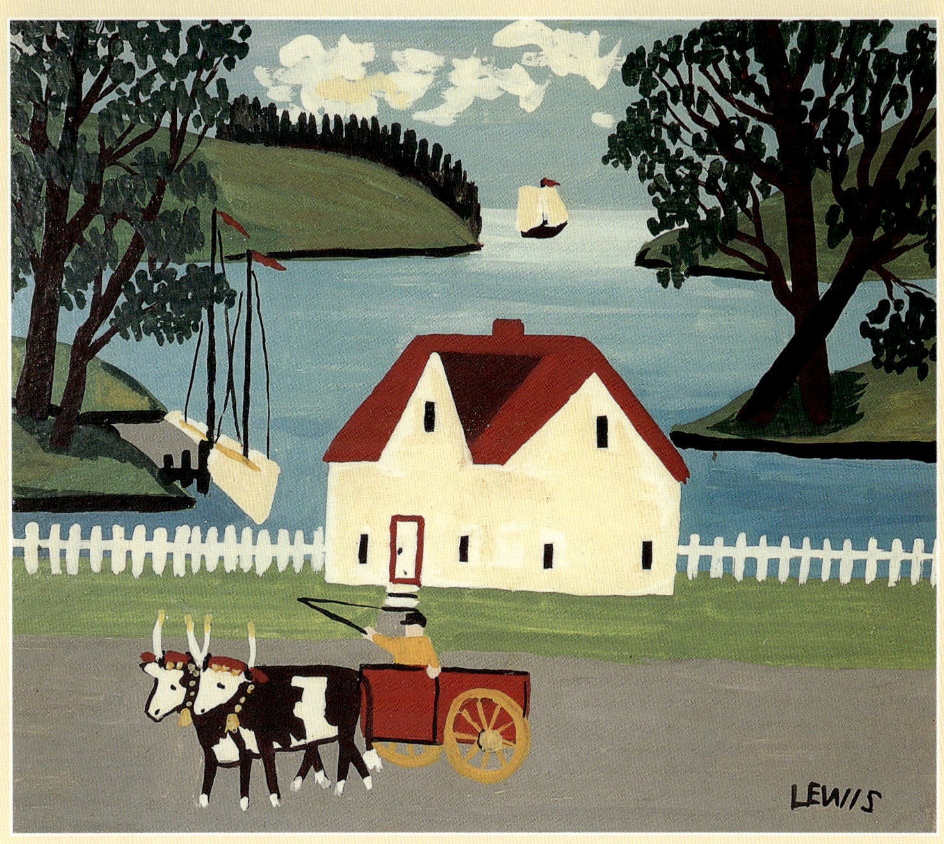

Wasn't he something else? He used to come along the road selling
fish. Keith knew him and gave slabwood from the mill to keep their
house warm in the winter. Ev wasn't quite all there. He came over
to my friend's house, and she had a shortsleeve dress on. He put
his hand on her arm: "Oh what a lovely arm!" But Keith always
gave him wood, as long as he had the mill. And the slabwood
would fit right into the old stove. A winter's wood,
that was a big thing.

Bert Potter, Interview, Plympton, NS, 1996

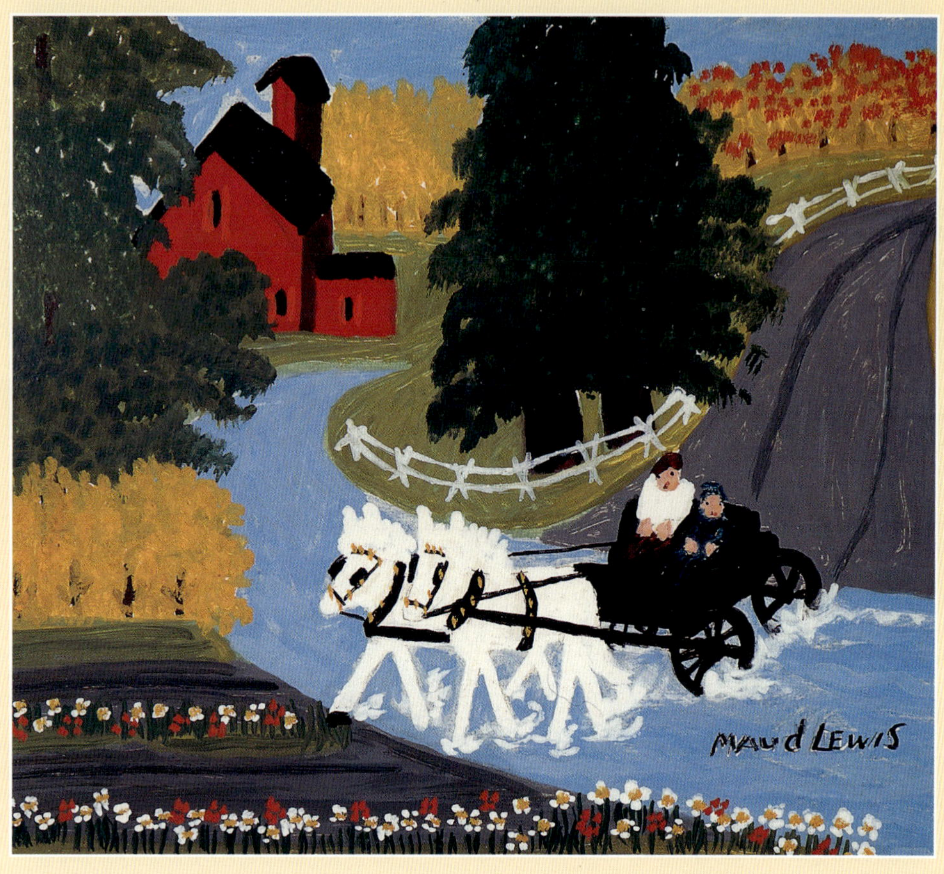

*I think probably Maud would be happy to think her paintings
were still in existence and that people care about them.*

Floss Lewis, Interview, Digby, NS, 1997

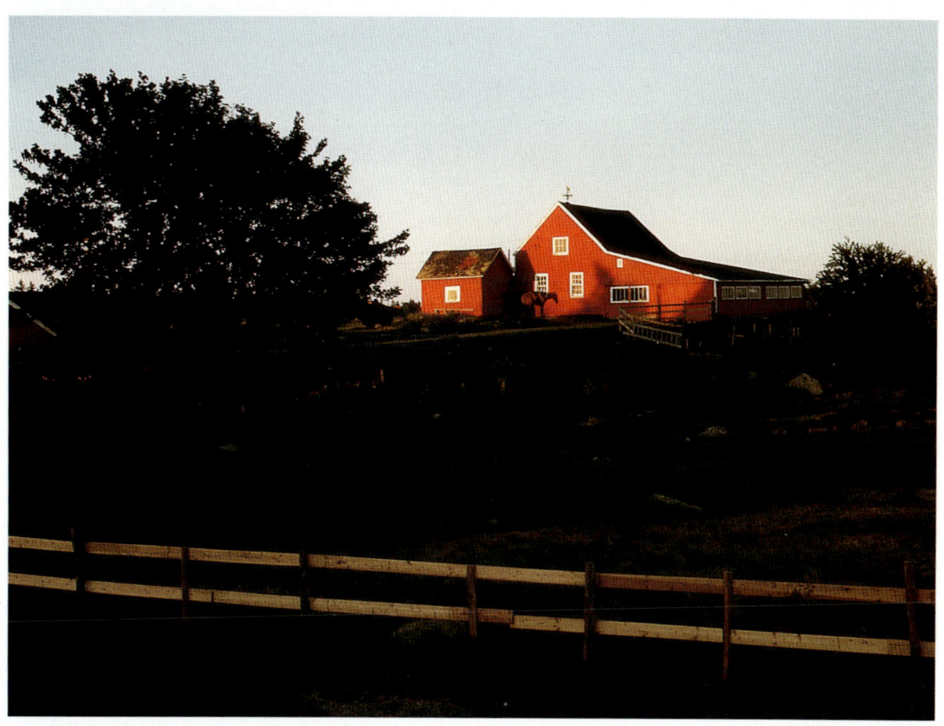

I didn't drive her home. I walked with her as far as the railroad underpass, 'cause it was dark. And let her walk the rest of the way alone. The next day I passed her on the road but I didn't pick her up. Well, a couple of days later she come down again, and that time I drove her home. And then we was married, and she come here to live.

Everett Lewis, Interview, Marshalltown, NS, 1975

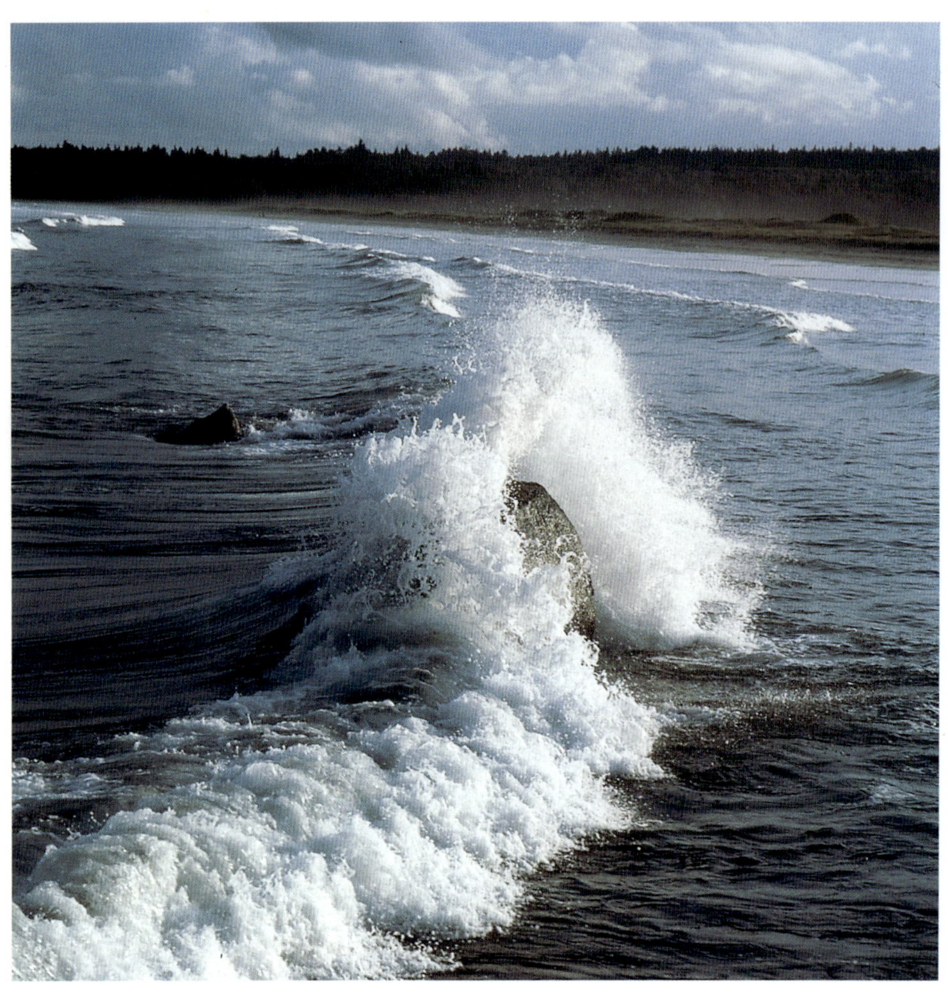

*Maud Lewis, who began her painting by doing Christmas cards,
loved to paint so much that she painted on anything, covered card-
board boxes, the staircase, the mirrors, the windows, the kitchen
stove, the blinds, the doors and many other objects.
Passers-by could see the cottage decorated with
painted flowers, birds and butterflies.*

Digby Courier, March 8, 1979

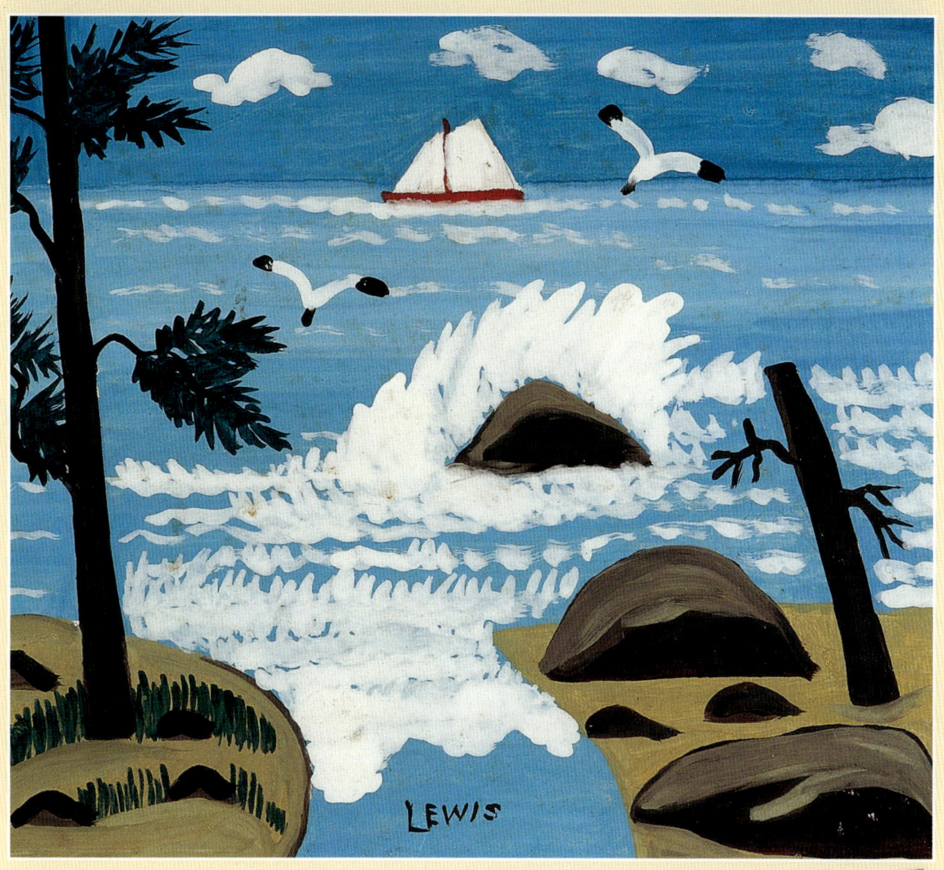

She didn't get out much. Maybe for a little walk. She couldn't do much, her hands were all crippled up. What she could do was, she could paint. So she would sit in that corner and paint. Christmas cards. Sell them for five cents. Desperate.

Arthur Sullivan, Interview, Digby, NS, 1995

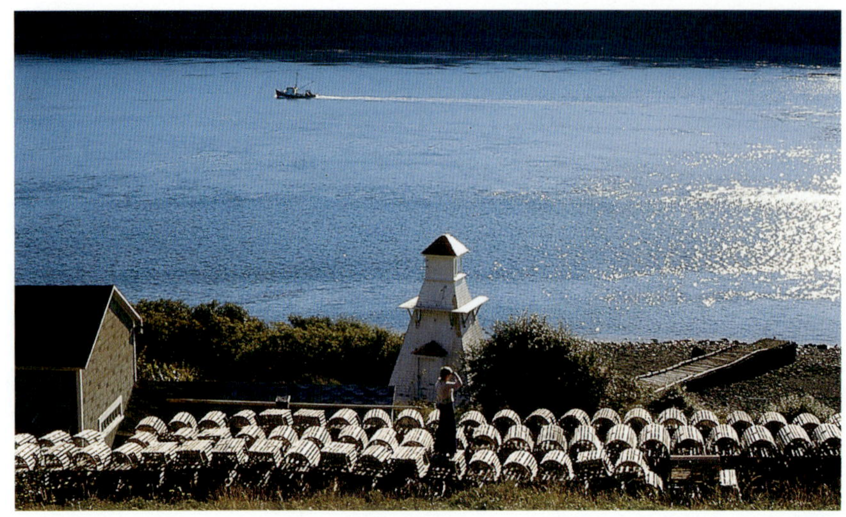

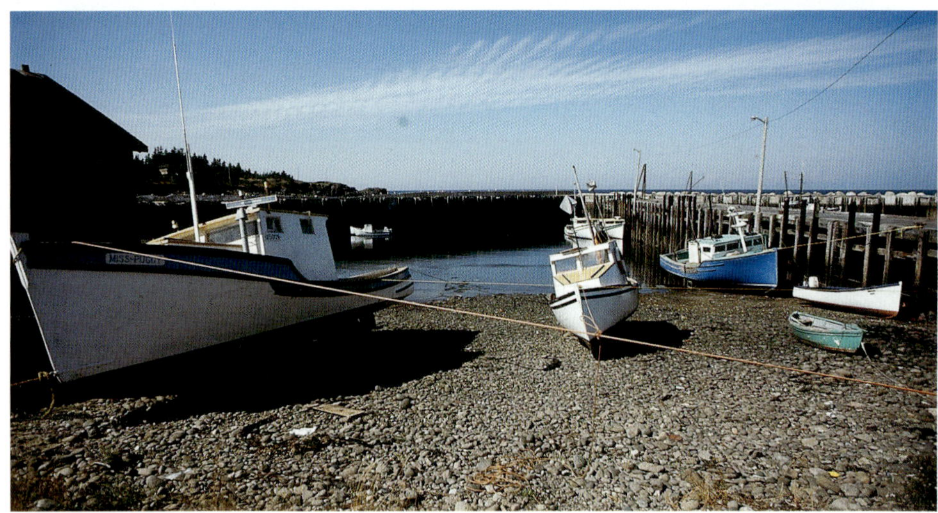

*Those summers in the Model T, that was when she travelled
with Ev, up hill and down dale. Down to the wharves to pick up
mackerel from the fishermen. Then up back of beyond to sell it.
But those summers, there was only a few. Ev sold the Model T to
Benny Haight I believe, and from then on it was common to see Ev
on his bicycle, "my wheel" as he called it. And Maud stayed home
and painted what she remembered for twenty or thirty years.*

Phillip Woolaver, Interview, Bear River, NS, 1994

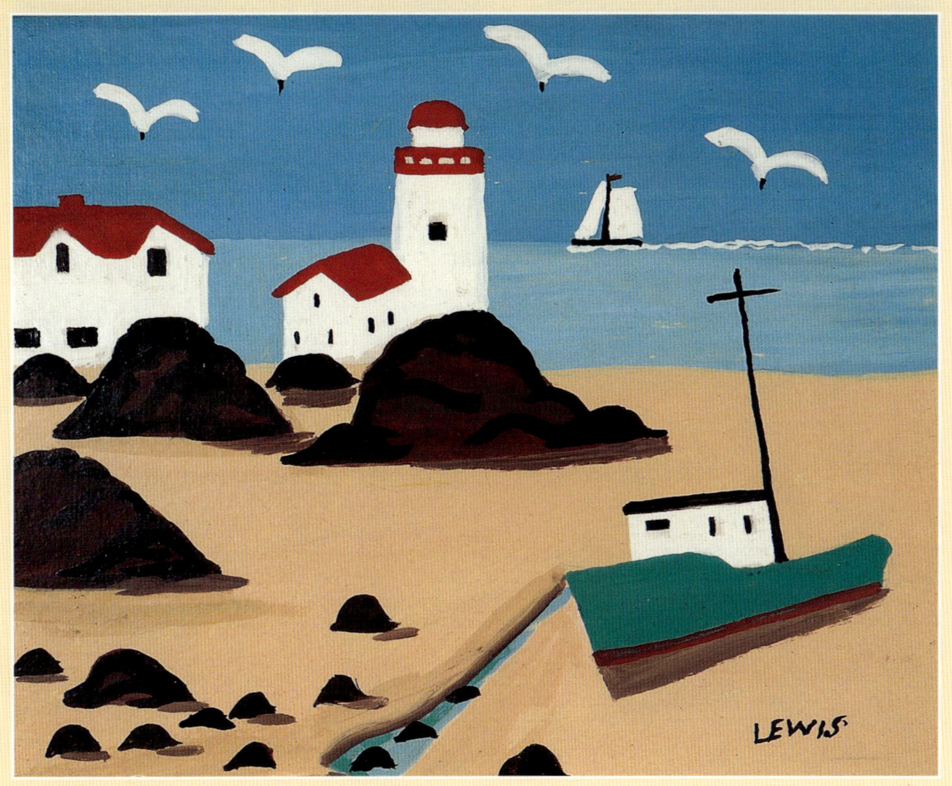

Mrs. Wallis, I can't keep up with the demand. I'll have to send these letters back.

Maud Lewis, as quoted in the *Digby Courier*, 1969

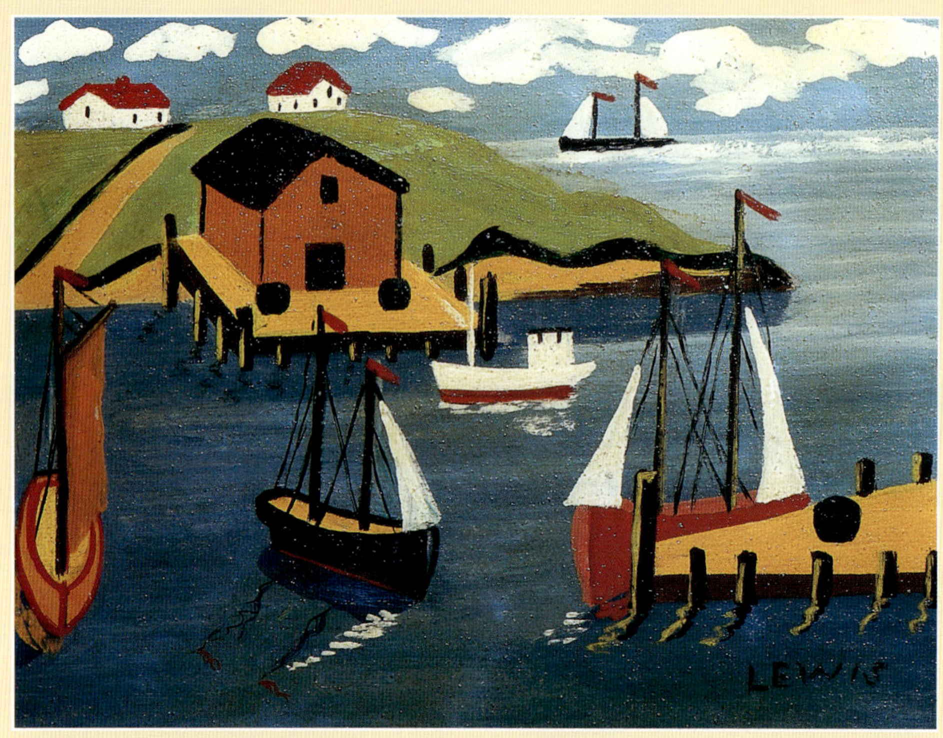

Ev Lewis was the best fish peddler in Digby County. He lived from the beach, clams, you know. Smelts when they were running. He never had much haddock but he had lots of mackerel because when they came, they came in clouds. And he got that old Model T and he kept it going.

Phillip Woolaver, Interview, Bear River, NS, 1995

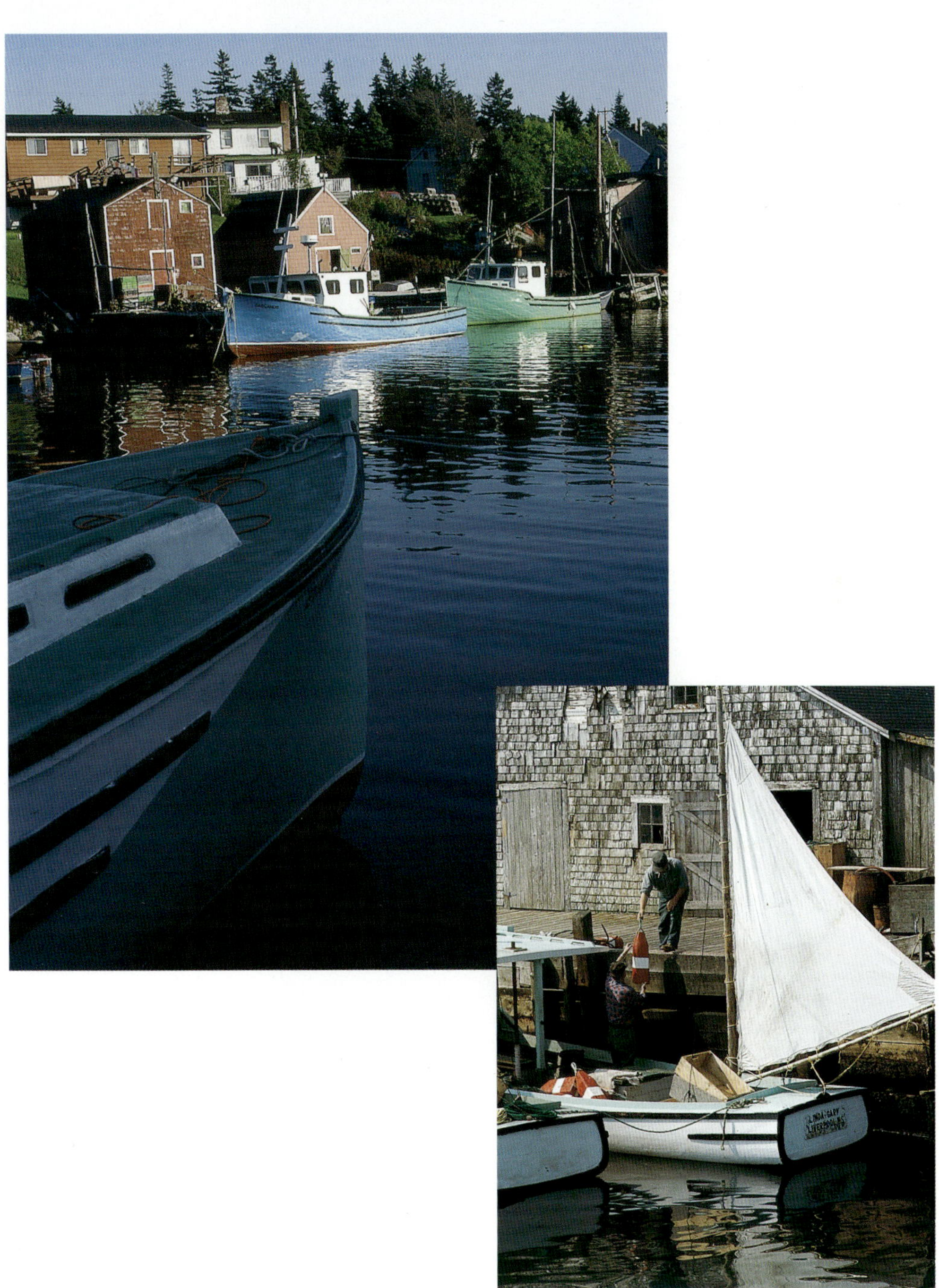

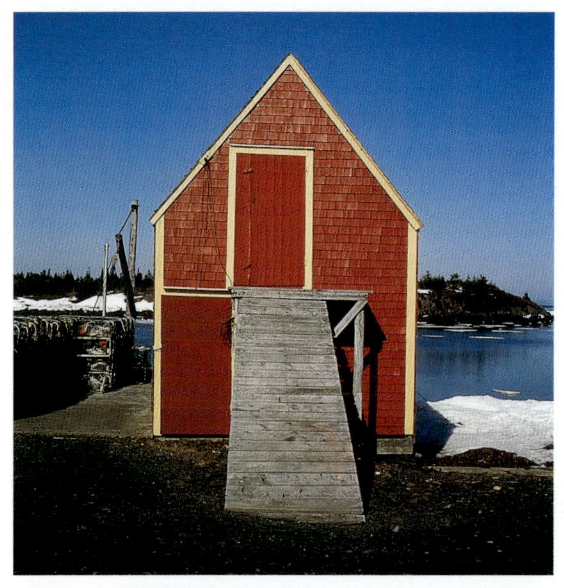

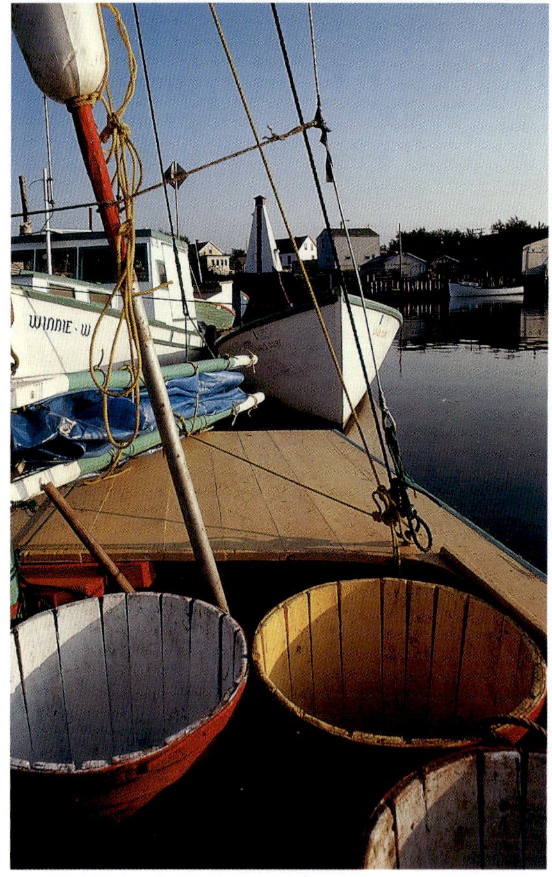

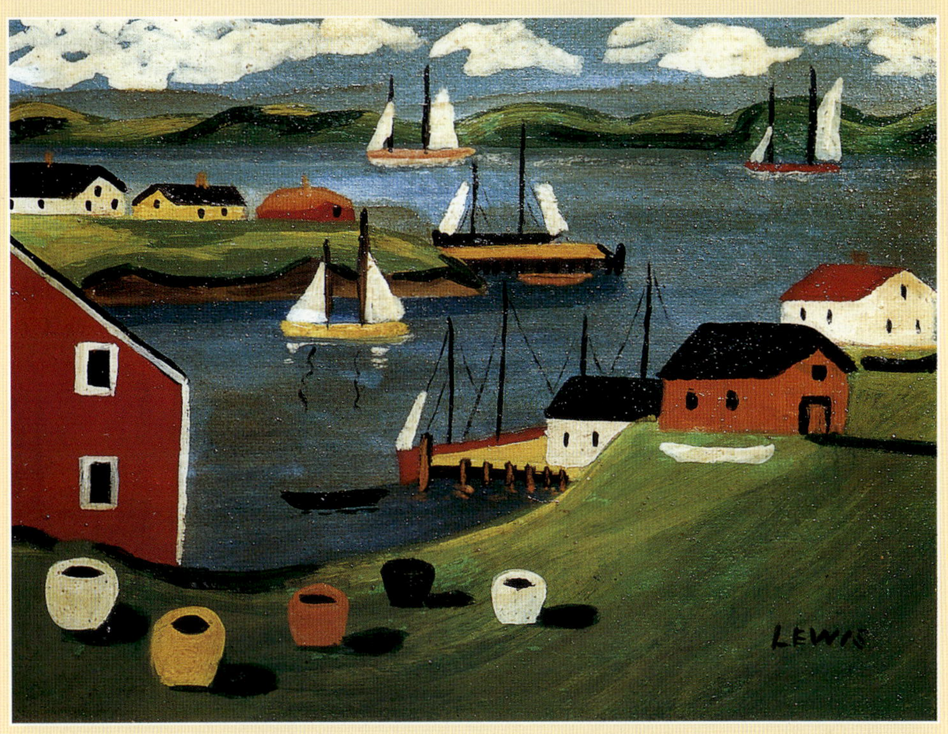

The first painting I bought was of fish in wooden barrels on the wharf—such a part of their lives. We first visited in the old house, a step from the road, and my last visit was when they were moving her house back from Highway No. 1 and she was in her trailer. Maud was usually sitting in her corner with her apron on, always cheerful and laughing as she talked. Our hearts went out to her as we saw her paint with her crippled hands.

Marilyn A. Margeson, Letter, 1994

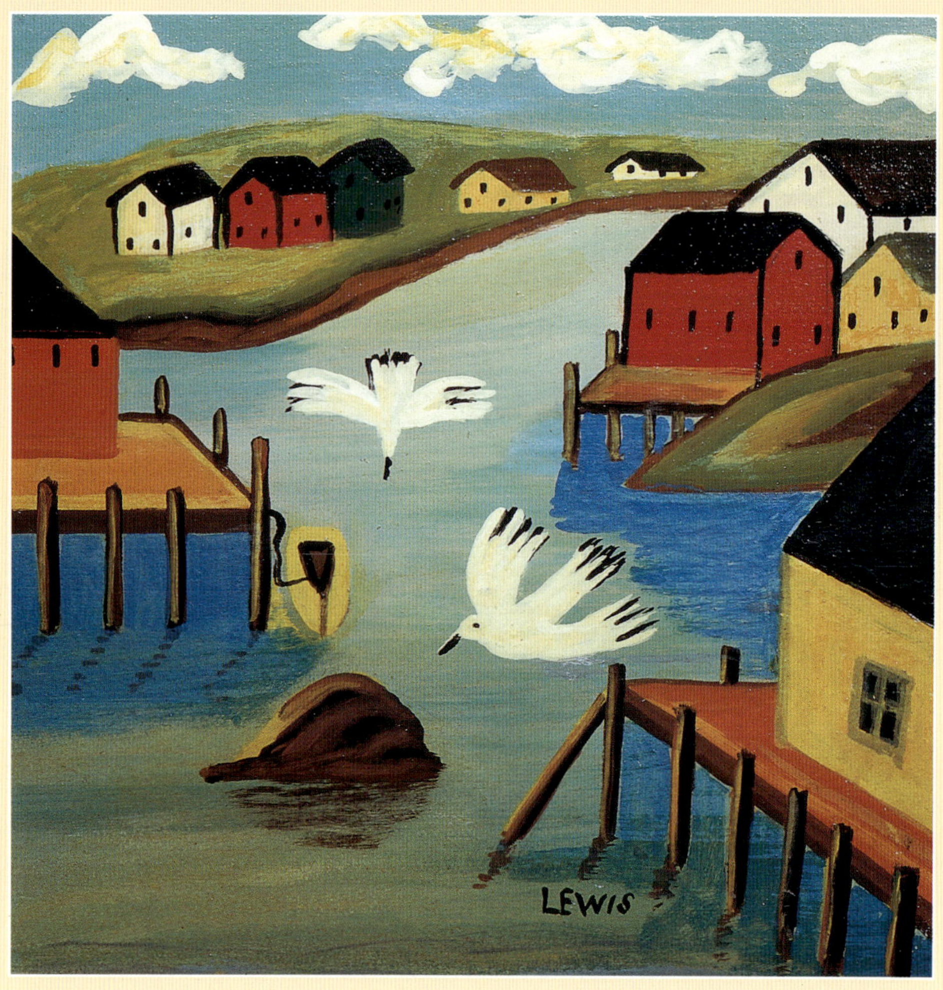

She lived at one time on Hawthorne Street overlooking Yarmouth Harbour. The activity was mostly based on the waterfront. Boats from Boston, fleets in the early days, the old square-rigged ships that came in here. And I believe with what she saw, the waterfront, with the oxen going by, the horses, the two trains ... and the ships and boats and fishing, these things impressed her and were so impressive on her mind that even when she started painting they were still foremost in her mind and that, I believe, is why we have so many of her paintings of oxen and the horses and the boats and ships and seagulls.

Nate Bain, Interview, Yarmouth, NS, 1997

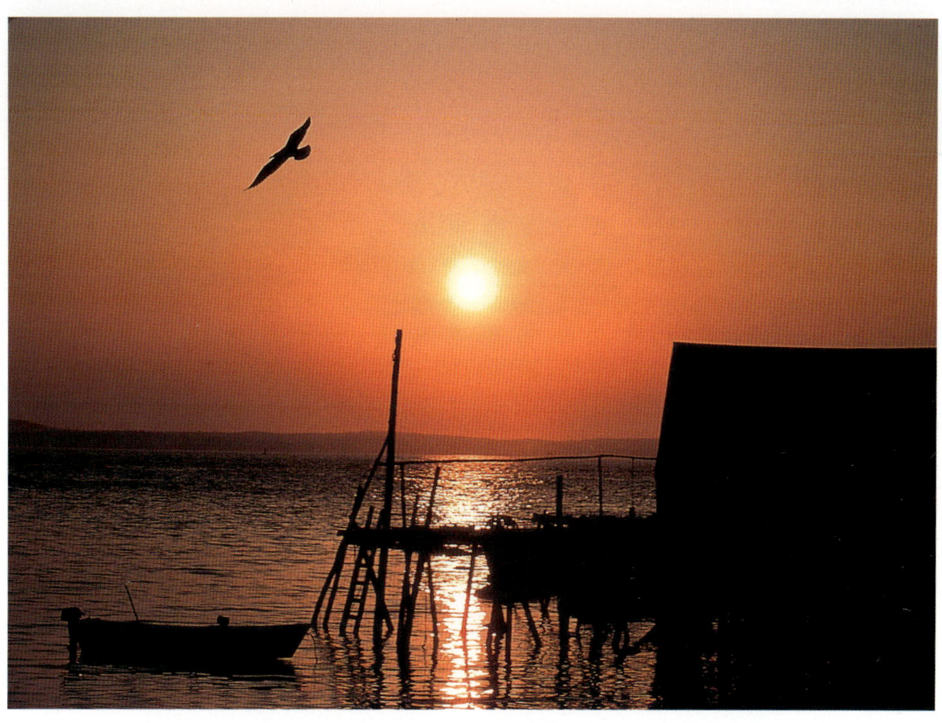

Paul Wilson says Ev's Model T was the best one in the province; he says he was surprised he couldn't smell a trace of fish in the vehicle despite peddling most every day. Paul says Ev must have scrubbed it clean every day because he tried to find a fish smell there many times when Ev wasn't looking. He never did. Ev was fussy about things like that, maybe that's why some people thought he was hard to get along with.

Phillip Woolaver, Letter, Bear River, NS, 1997

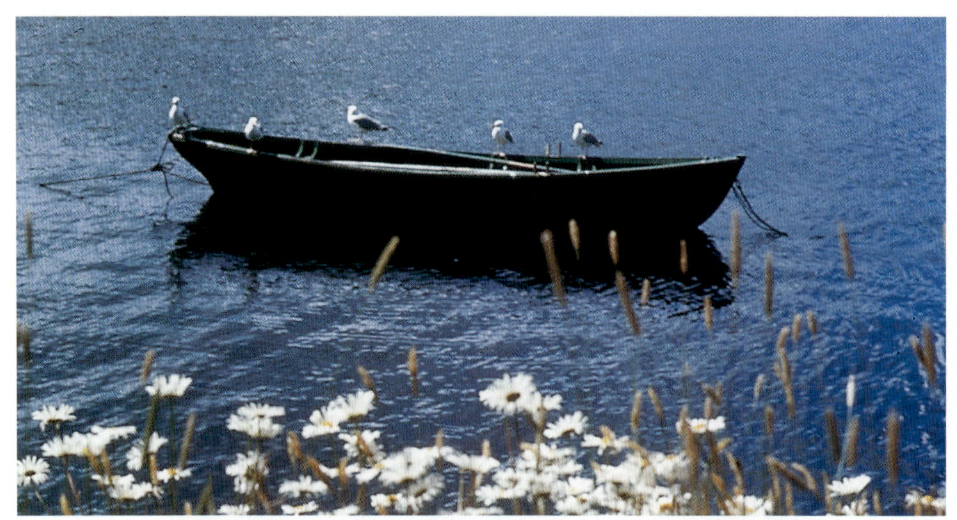

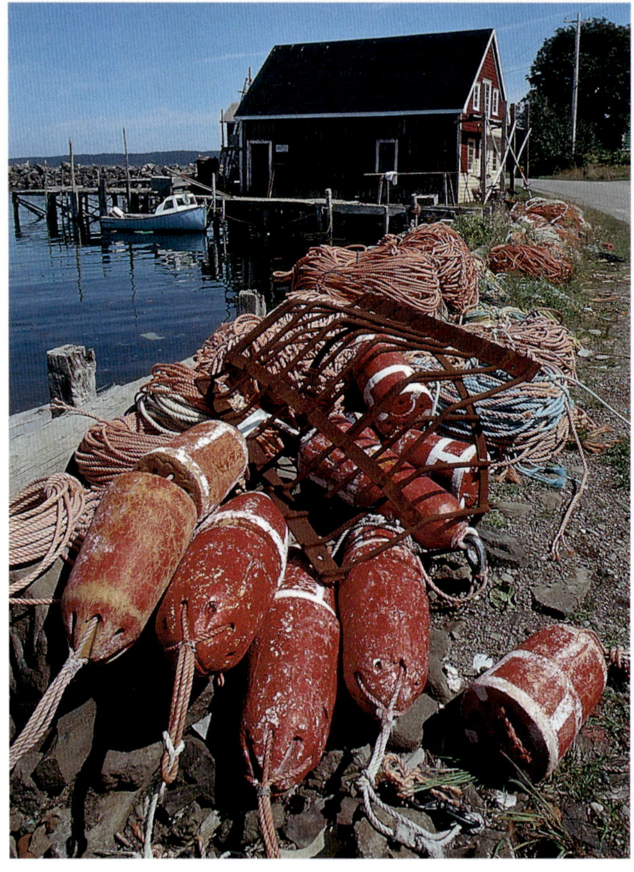

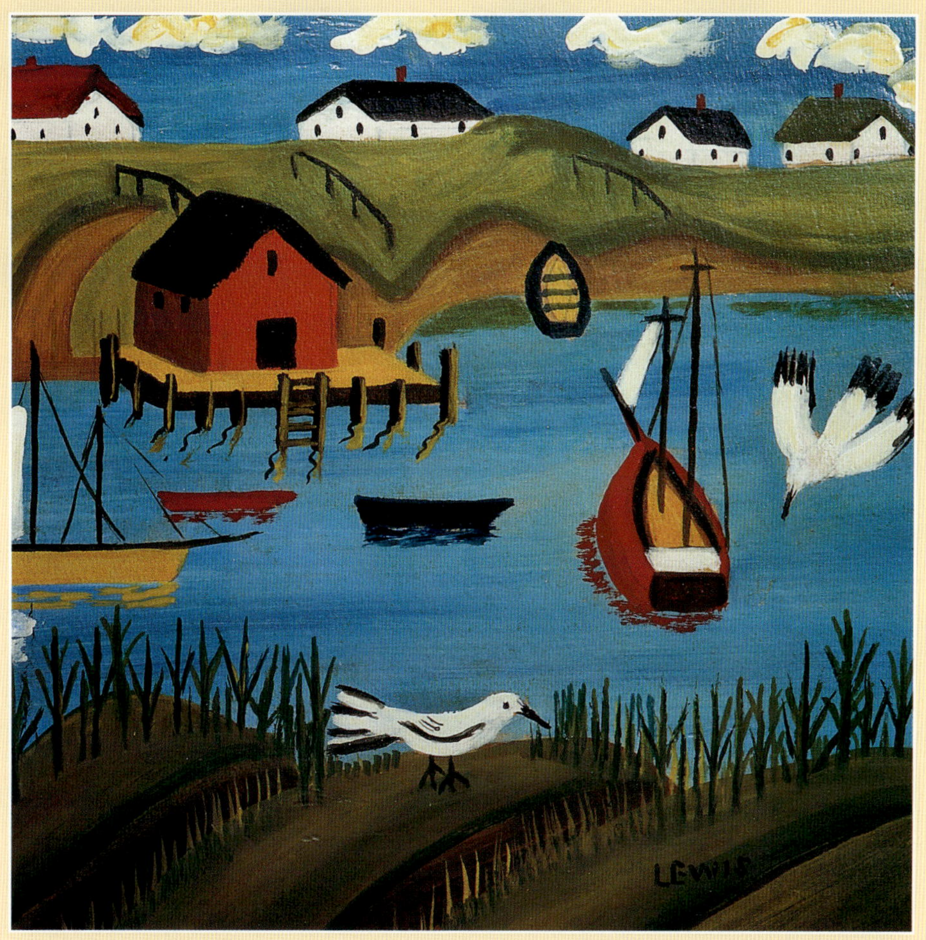

Yes, she lived there in Digby with Aunt Ida, a very Christian
woman. Maud stayed there 'cause Ida always had a hand out to
help the family. Until Maud walked out on the railroad tracks,
heard about Mr. Everett Lewis living alone. She wanted a home of
her own. She walked out on the tracks and knocked on the door. I
heard my Grampy talk about it a lot. One time, Maud was in the
hospital and I went in to see her. It was winter. It would break
your heart. She was lying on a lambskin.

Mrs. Basil Outhouse, Interview, Digby, NS, 1995

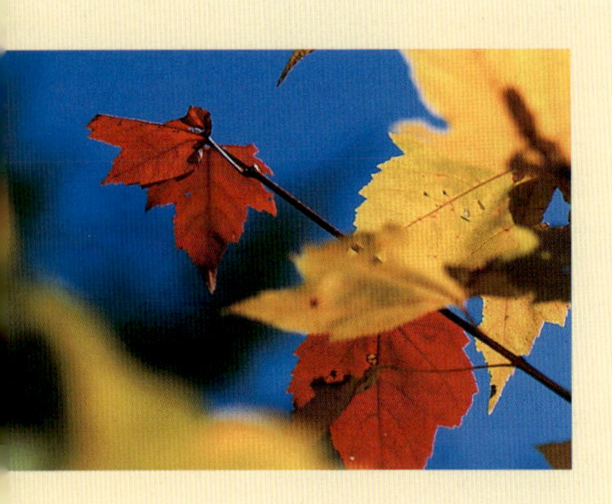

THE VILLAGE OF BEAR RIVER has the distinction of belonging to two counties, Digby and Annapolis. As the name implies, a river runs through it—a great tidal river that runs green when the salt water flows upstream, and blue when the tide departs. Families who live on the east bank send their children, and their taxes, to Annapolis Royal, the oldest town in North America. Those who live on the west side, send them to Digby, home of the round-the-world sailor Joshua Slocum.

Ev and Maud travelled through the hills around Bear River making his deliveries, and here we find the source of many of her landscapes; in particular, one entitled "Above Kniffin's Hollow." From the Annapolis side, the artist looked down to the river and across to the farm of Maud's patron, Judge Woolaver. The scene today is exactly as Maud painted it in 1954. Even the birch tree in the foreground is still standing, although it is bigger. Late in October, the bark is the same dappled black and paper white, and its autumn leaves the same unvariegated yellow that Maud saw and remembered. It is said that the Kniffins no longer live in the Hollow, but the ghosts of the little Kniffins still inhabit the brook that drops into the river.

Much of what Maud painted for her visitors derived from commercial postcards. Her commissioned landscapes, however, feature specific locations. Her paintings of steam locomotives look back to the time when she was a young woman in Yarmouth. Her neighbours remember her keeping a schedule by which she would emerge from

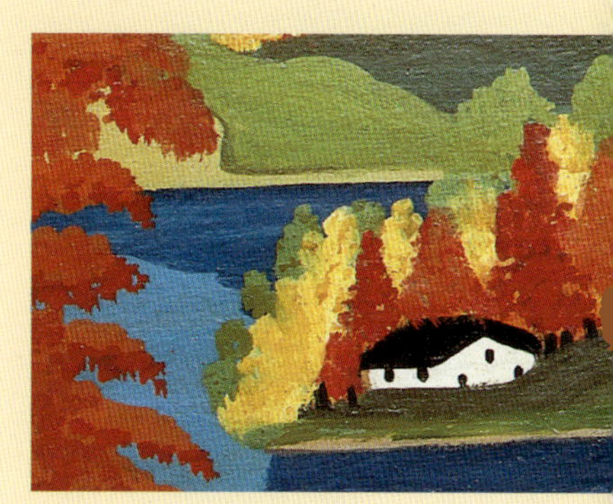

her house on Hawthorne Street and raise a hand in time to greet the train's arrival, a hundred yards below. The engineer, "Oat" Stark of Digby, would toot the whistle. The brakeman would look up and wave as he swung on and off the moving boxcars.

Maud's gift with colour was never more true to nature than in her autumn paintings, when the trees around her turned from green to red, yellow, orange, and brown.

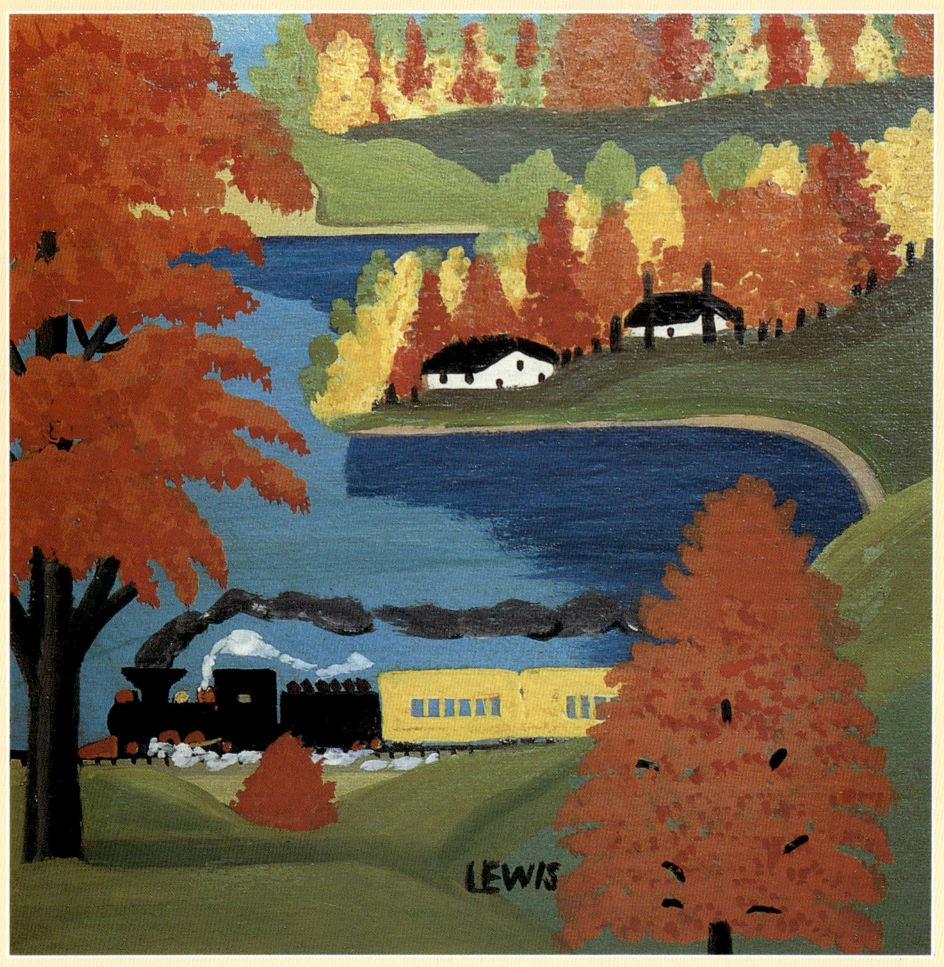

Maud liked railroad songs. Wilf Carter. Jimmy Rodgers. I bought
that little transistor radio … It was three dollars and ninety-nine
cents, no tax. And I took it to Maud and WWVA must have been
very powerful because you could get it no trouble. I can hear him
now, the announcer, "This is Dub-Yah, Dub-Yah, Vee, A—Wheeling,
West Virginia. You're gonna hear some good music this afternoon
ladies and gentlemen." And then the strumming, then the opening
of a beautiful ballad: "Come hear my story of heartaches and
sighs. I'm the prisoner who's lonely for my moonlight and skies."
She loved those songs like there was no tomorrow.

Phillip Woolaver, Interview, Bear River, NS, 1996

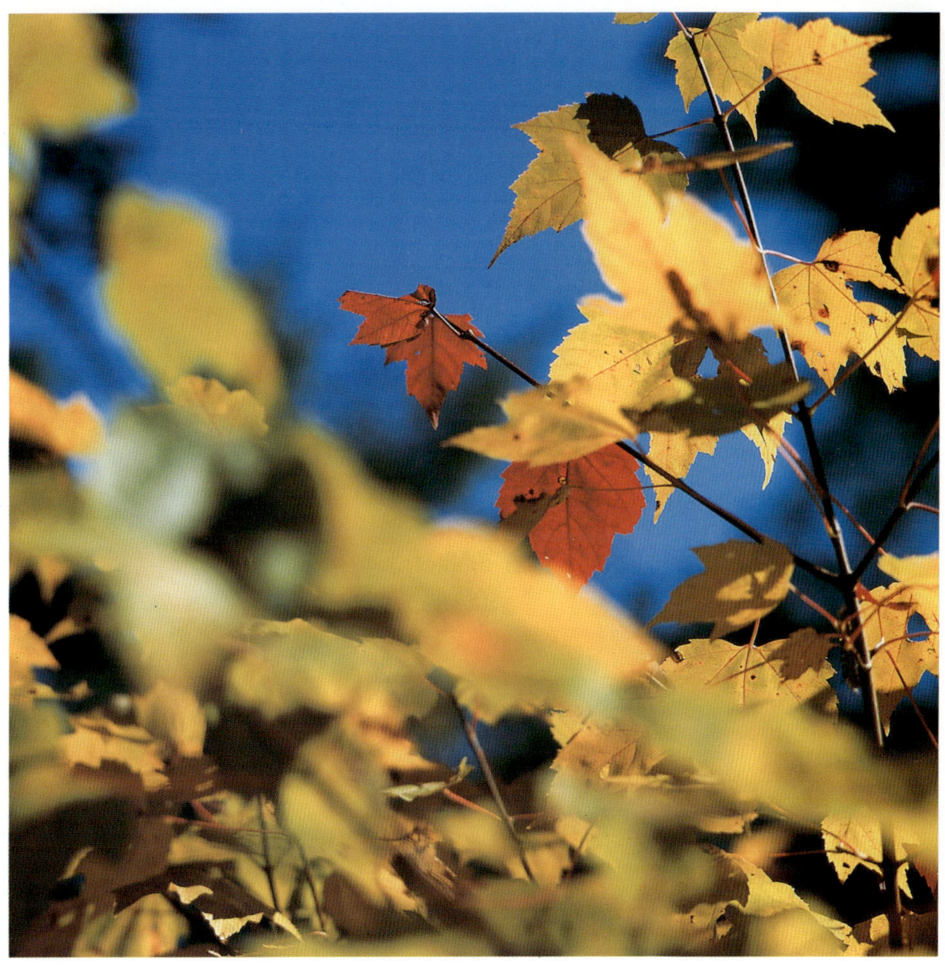

She also painted outdoor pictures when she took liberties with nature as it suited her. I have a winter scene where she has trees with green leaves and orange leaves and yellow leaves and so I said, Maud, but that's not possible. In mid-winter you don't have these colours. Oh yes, she said, you can, if you have an early snow-fall then you can have that. And I thought, yeah she's right. And she said, anyhow, it doesn't really matter. It looks nicer when you have different colours.

Cora Greenaway, Interview, Dartmouth, NS, 1997

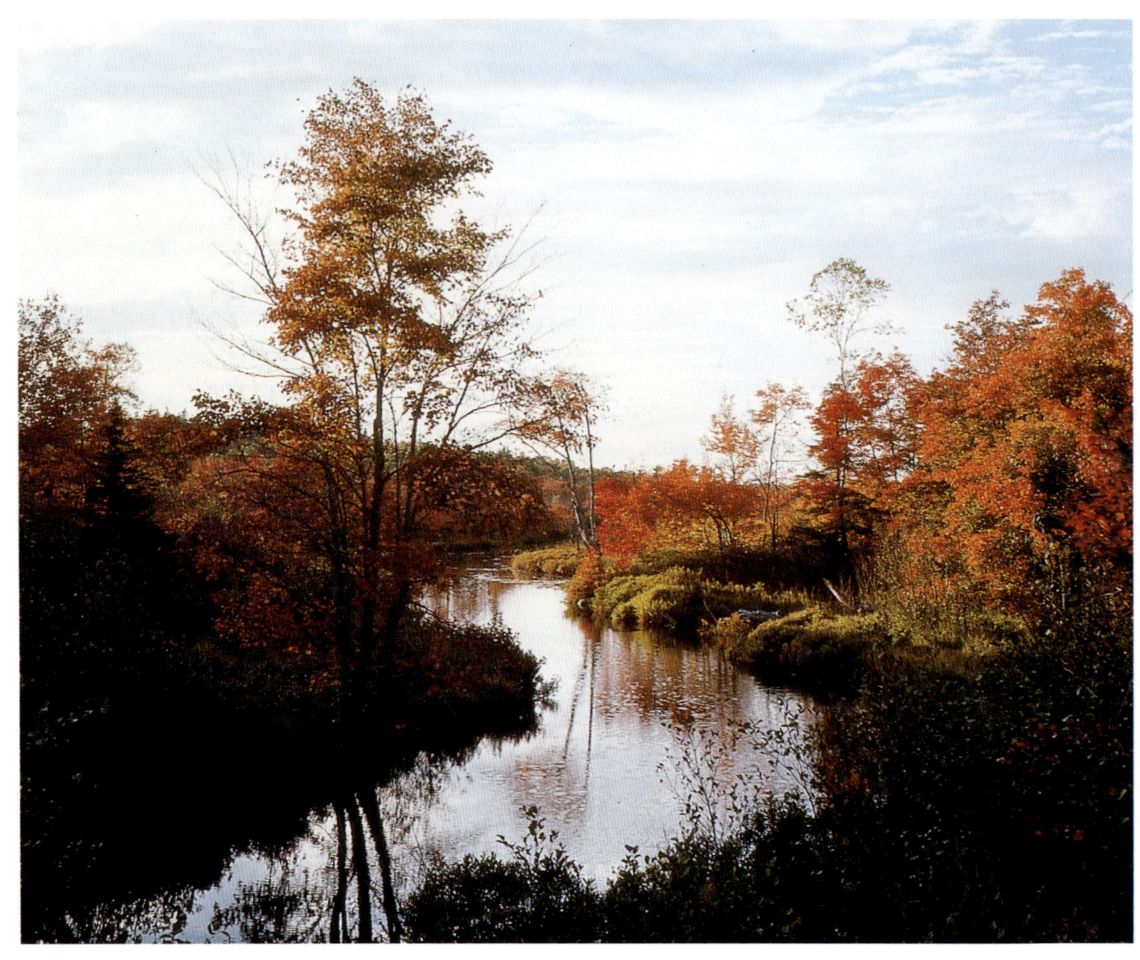

People don't understand how to create folk art. It's got to be basically from the heart and in your mind and your hand a bit because that's the thing that makes it. And they can't seem to project the simplicity of it, the crooked buildings and things out of proportion is how they see it. They're used to everything being stiff and meaning something. The folk art is pure simplicity and the people who buy folk art are hunting for simplicity.

Stephen Outhouse, Interview, Digby, NS, 1997

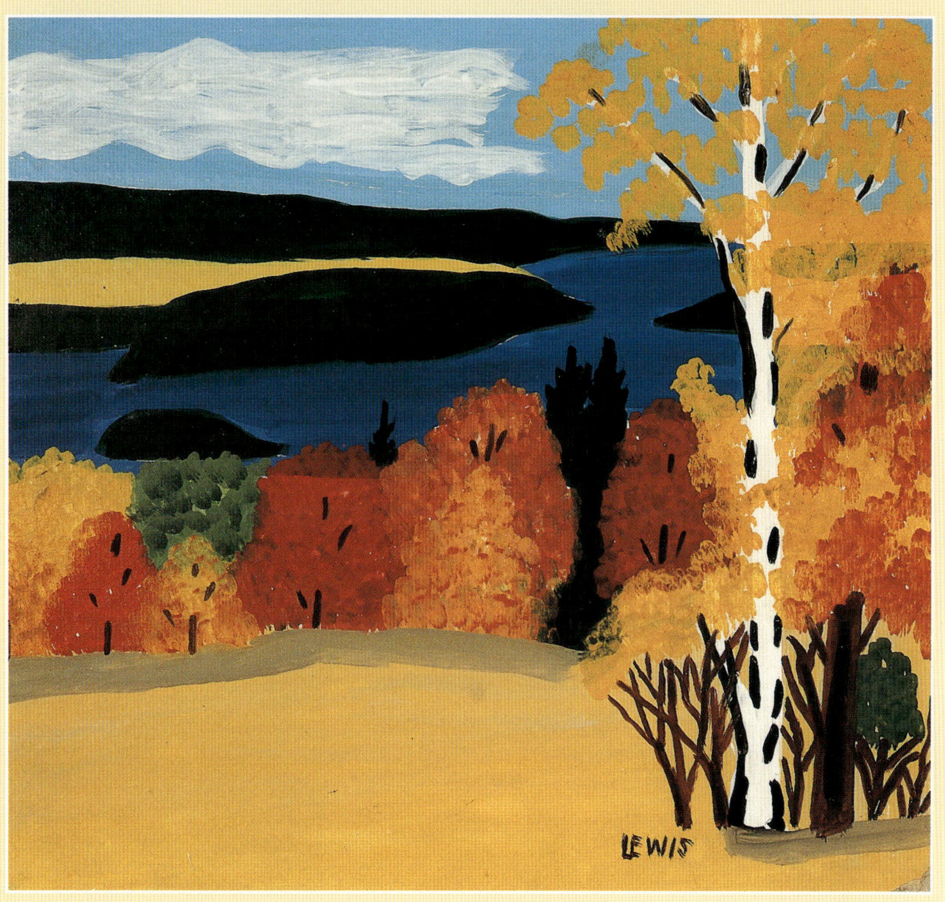

I think there's a great deal of joy in the paintings. They're certainly bright and they're colourful and always cheerful. Even today, some of the paintings are getting on for nearly fifty years old and they still look as fresh today as the day when they were painted.

Alan Deacon, Interview, Wolfville, NS, 1997

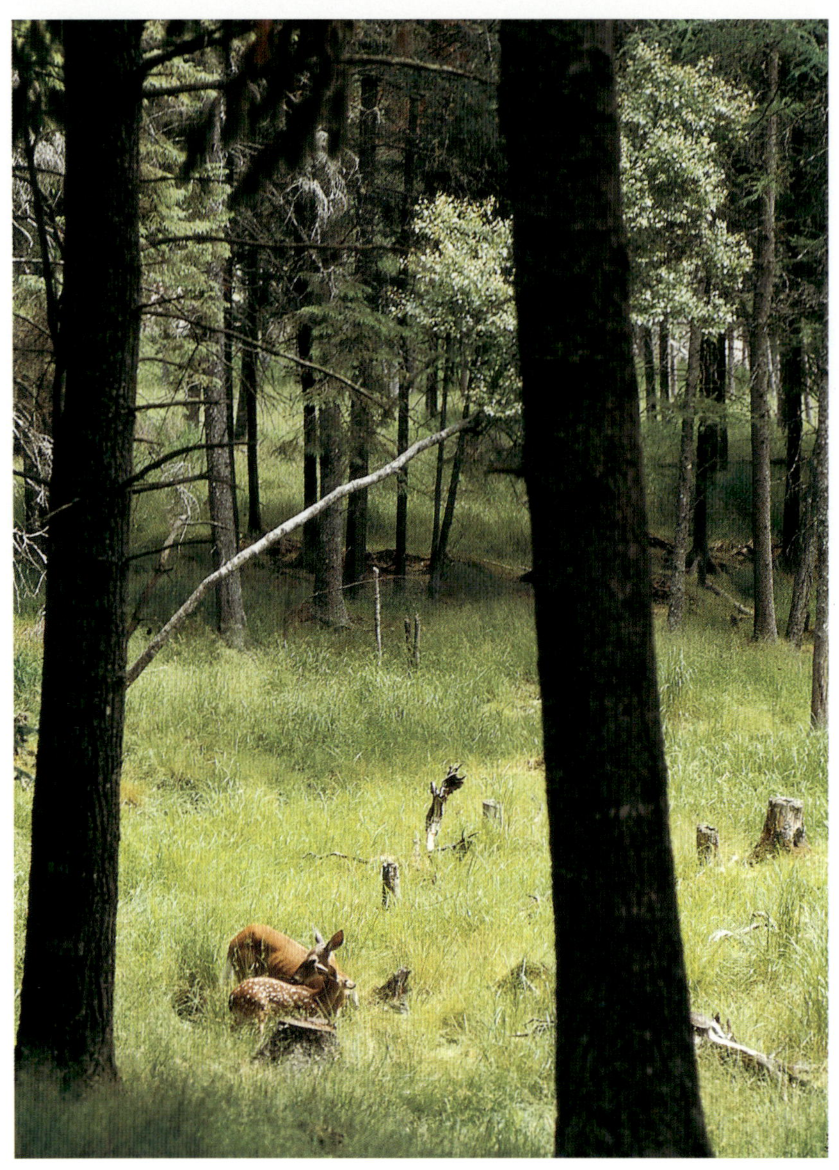

*Maud Lewis paints what we dream about. Most familiar are her
massive oxen with big, soulful eyes and long eyelashes.
Other subjects, all outdoor scenes, include Cape Island boats,
horses and sleighs, surreys, dogs, cats, maple sugaring and gentle
sloping hillsides with cows grazing among the flowers. She did not
often raise her head, but those who knew her have said that when
she did, her clear blue-grey eyes lit up her face like candles.*

Gretchen Pierce, *Mail Star*, July 5, 1974

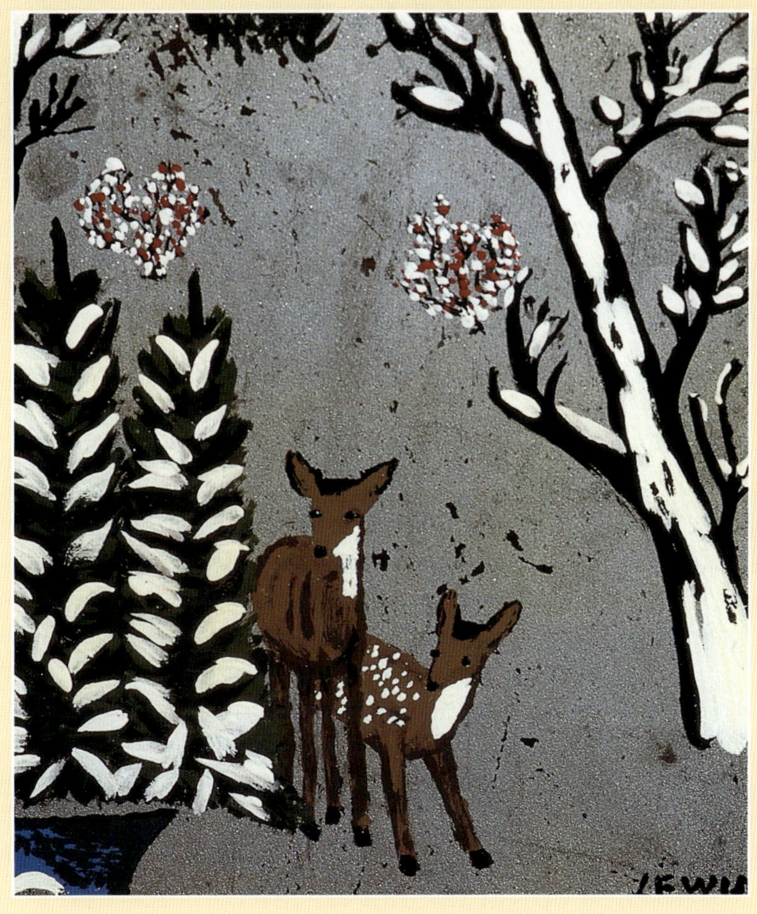

"*Everett, where is the one I did yesterday with the oxen in it?*"

"*Well, Maud, you know yourself that doctor fellow from
Digby took it off. You gave it to him.*"

"*Hmph. Horses are nice.
Or how about this here deer in the woods?*"

Maud and Everett Lewis, CBC *Telescope*, 1965

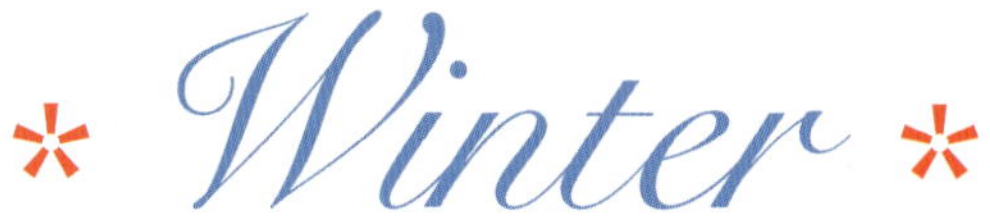

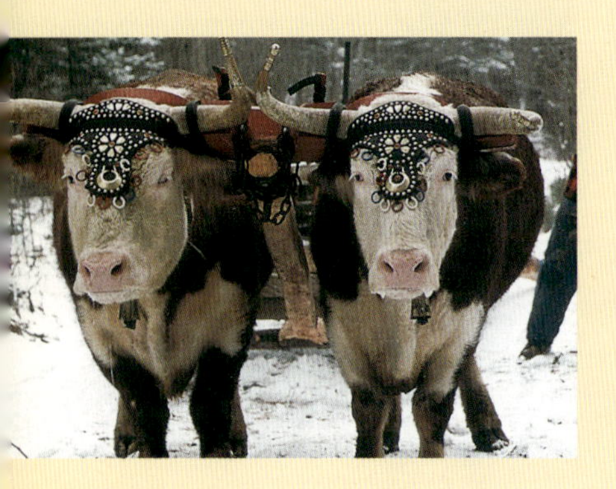

I

N MAUD'S DAY, winter was a working season. As soon as the harvest ended, men turned their hands to woods work and lobster fishing, both of which provided cash incomes. Much of the work in summer and autumn did not pay. You planted a garden to save on groceries and you parcelled out seaweed to the spent fields to avoid buying fertilizer, but winter offered the promise of real money.

The state of the country roads in the 1930s was poor. An unpaved road in Nova Scotia could be a muddy quagmire in the spring, and a dusty, bumpy discomfort in the summer. The roads levelled out in the fall and froze slick and smooth in winter, making it easier to haul a load of logs or zip up the lane. So when Everett Lewis ventured into the woods in winter, the firewood and logs were sitting along the roads waiting for the first good freeze-up. It was then that Ev could bring home the winter's supply; or, being Ev, have his neighbours bring it to him. It was also then that the paper mills hired a winter's crew and the men left their farms and lobster boats to go to the woods camps.

It is characteristic of Maud that she
was more interested in painting the
oxen than the teamster. Many details
are included on these placid beasts,
including a red or golden heart in the
decorative brass—the same heart she
painted on the door of her house.

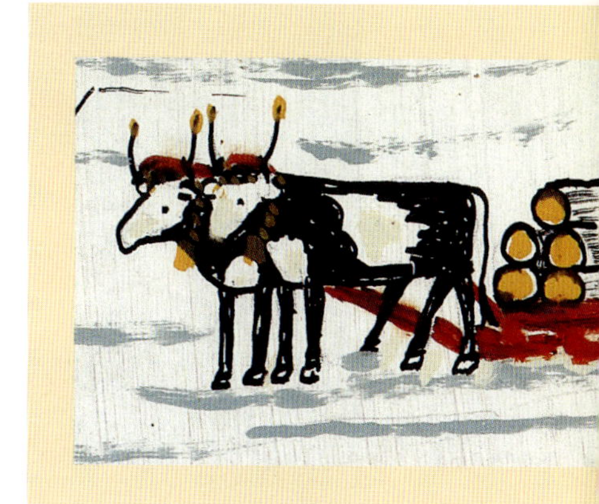

The Christmas holiday temporarily
broke the winter's work, and Maud's
paintings recollect the season of neighbourly visits by horse
and sleigh. She painted many Christmas cards, sometimes
copying other printed cards to celebrate the holiday. The
ones that date from her younger years in Yarmouth, when
she and her mother painted together, show groups of
people—especially carolers and skaters.

One of Maud's most exceptional paintings is a winter
nocturnal scene of a landscape and a house in Bear River
East. The colour and the style are unusual, but the place is
quite authentic, with one exception—the bridge is one that
Maud invented. The tranquility of this scene is like the deep
quiet after a snowstorm, an event with which Maud would
have been only too familiar.

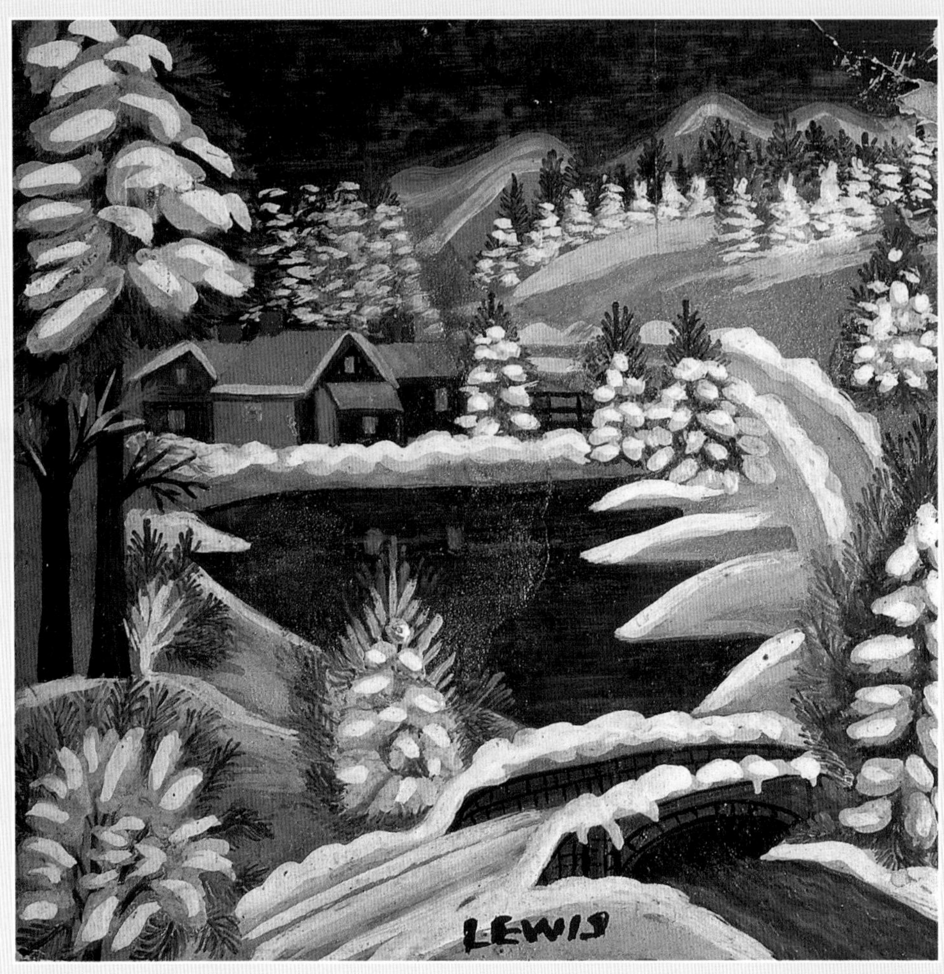

Inside the house everything with a flat surface was painted with flowers and butterflies (even the black cook stove was decorated). We were invited to have a seat and some tea, but as Everett wasn't much of a housekeeper, there wasn't a chair that wasn't covered with books, clothes and paint supplies to sit on anyway. We talked with Maud for a while and she said she painted from what she could remember from years past, as she couldn't get out anymore.

Mrs. Carol Hill, Letter, 1994

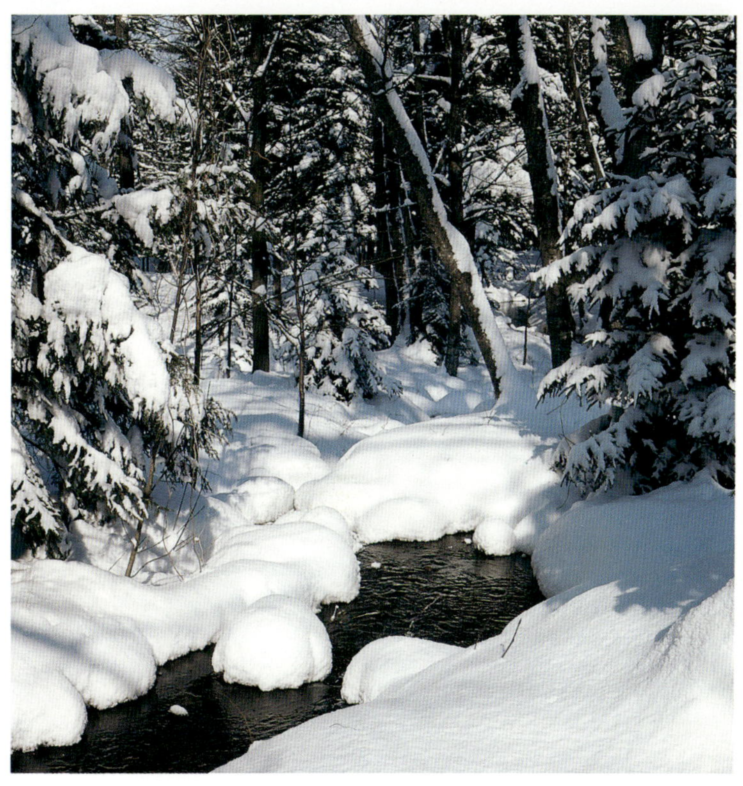

My family and I were on the way to the U.S. for a week or two, and stopped at Maud's house. We were much taken with the way she had decorated the downstairs with paintings of flowers on the walls and woodwork. I asked her if she would be prepared to paint a picture for me. She was reluctant because she had other orders to fill, but eventually agreed.

Roy E. George, Letter, 1996

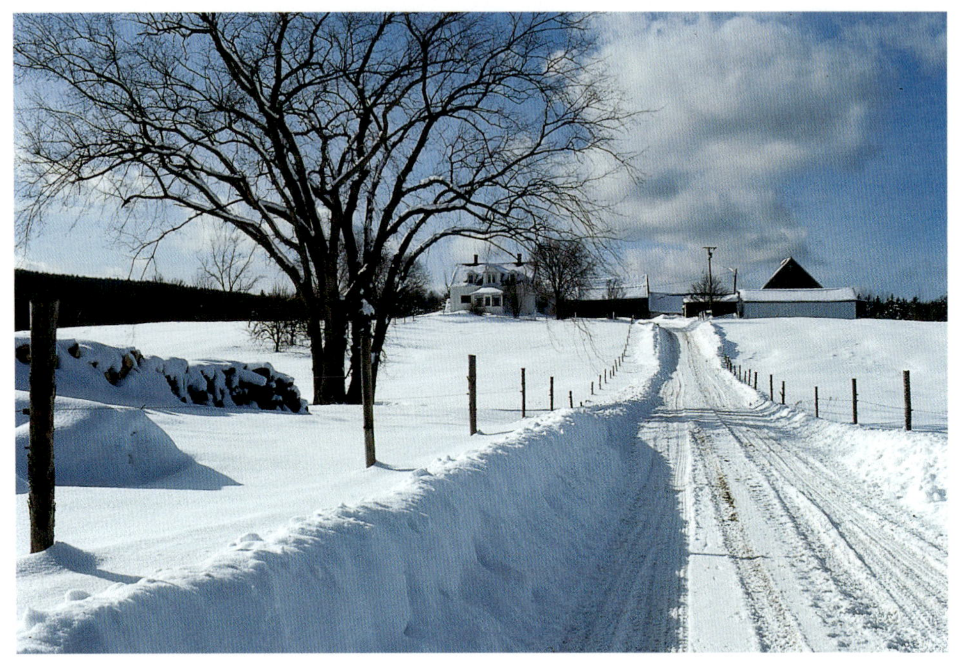

*What I'd like is a little more room. Like to have a trailer, couldn't
afford that! I'm contented here. I ain't much for traveling anyway.
As long as I've got a brush in front of me, I'm all right.*

Maud Lewis, CBC *Telescope,* 1965

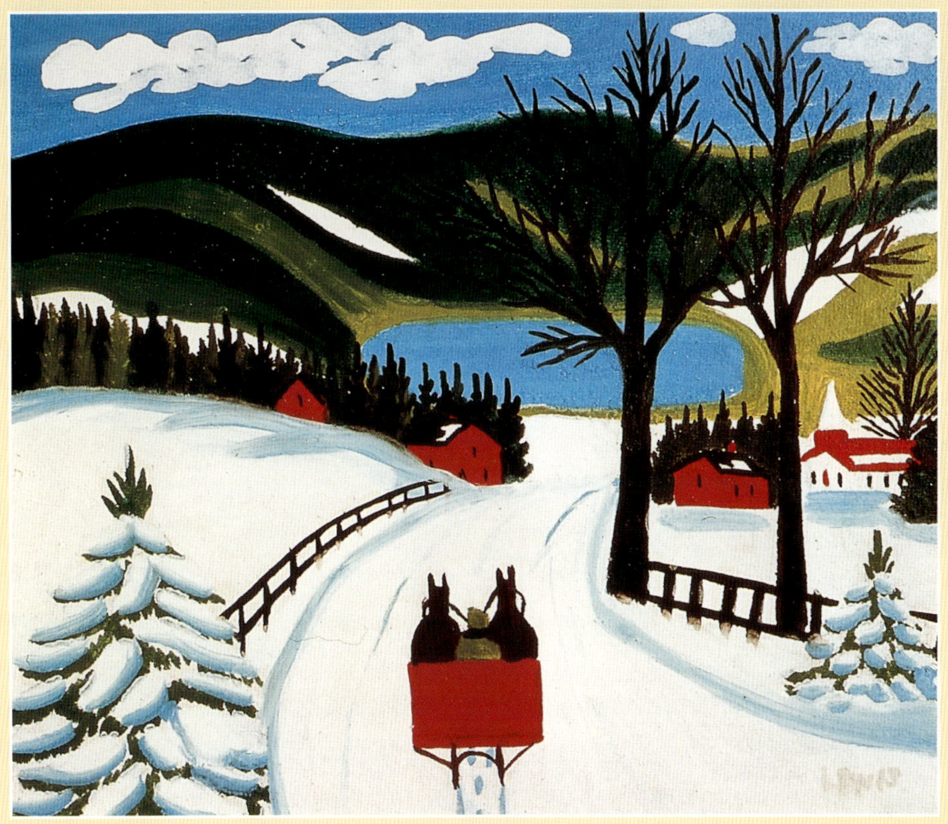

My husband and I stopped into the house the next summer and purchased another picture to give to my father as a Xmas gift. Again, we were allowed only one to save a supply for others.

Carol Hill, Coldbrook, NS, Letter, 1994

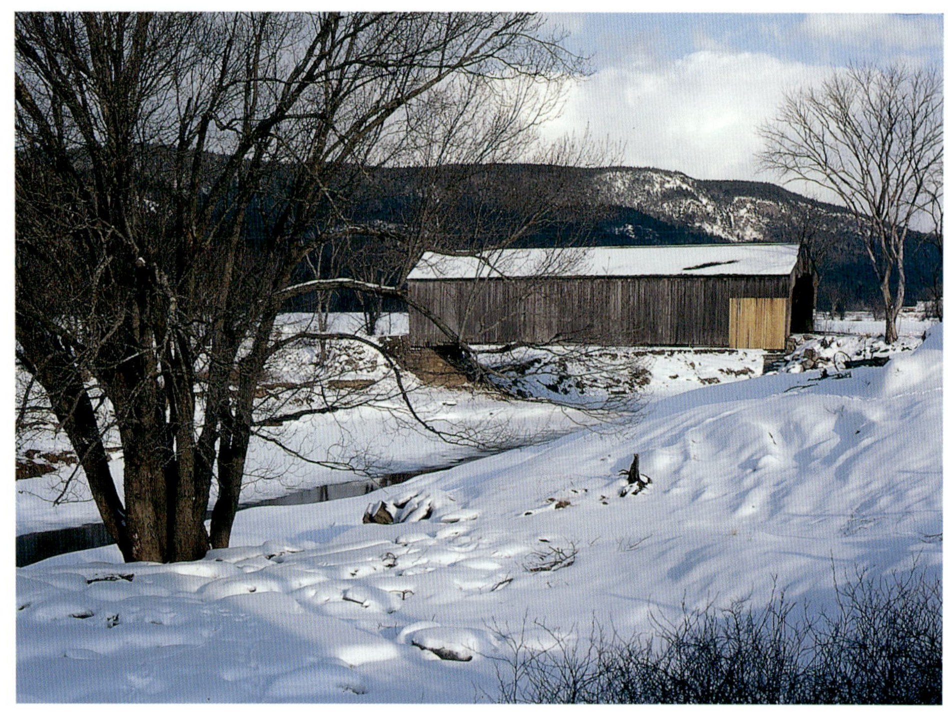

She painted all winter. That's about all she done. 'Course she did the cooking too. She did her other work and painting. Kept her busy! She kept me busy too, cutting the boards.

Everett Lewis, Interview, Marshalltown, NS, 1972

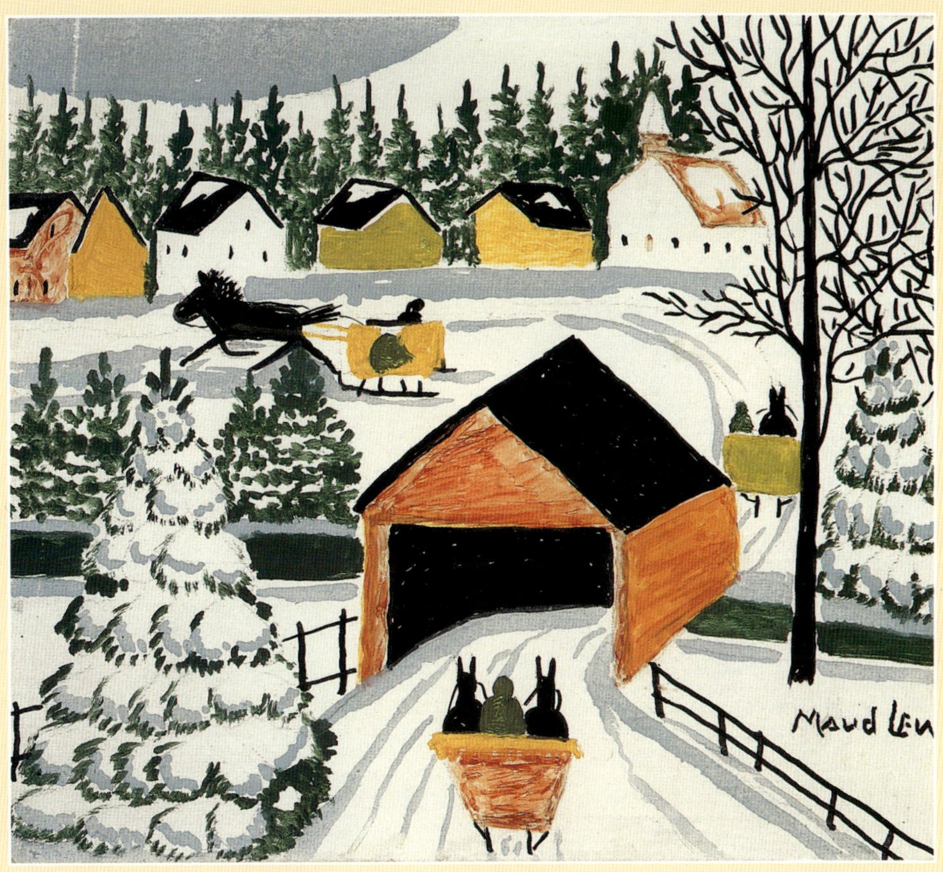

The most striking thing about Maud is her eyes. Small and some-
what crippled by arthritis, she sits huddled with thin brown arms
crossed on her chest like willow branches and smiles shyly
as a school girl from under her broad forehead and
cap of grey-brown hair.

Murray Barnard, *Star Weekly*, July 10, 1965

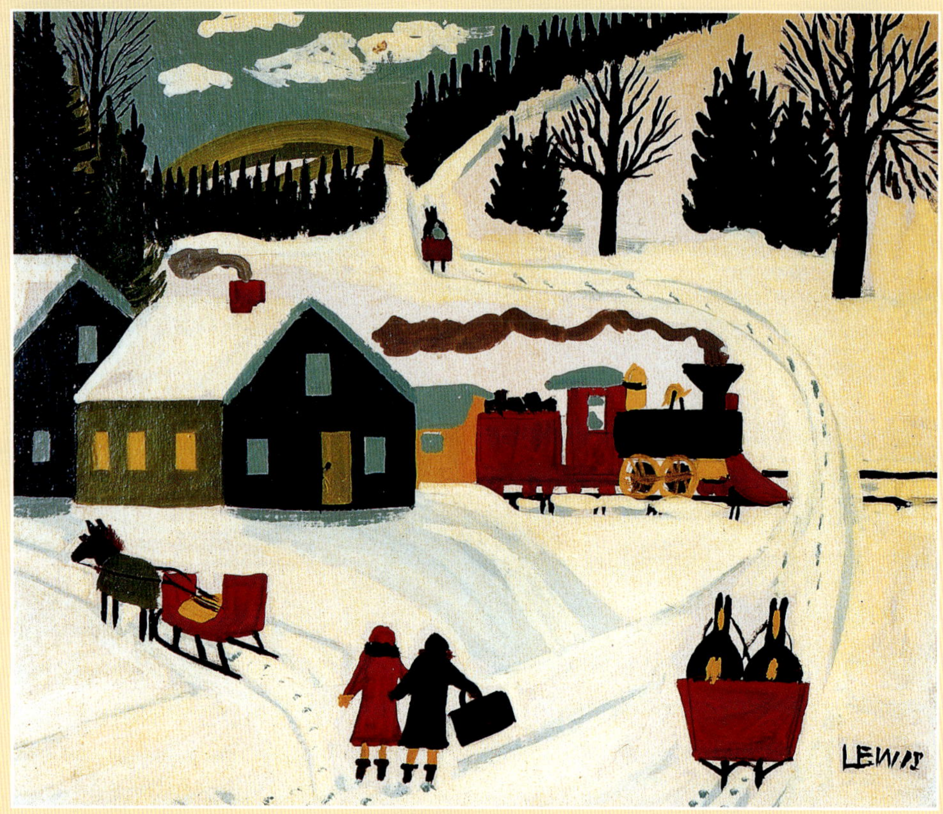

She tried to take the complication out of her life, by the way she seen life around her. The rural Digby area. Because she had a terrible life, she made it as simple and calm and peaceful and bright as she could.

Stephen Outhouse, Interview, Brighton, NS, 1997

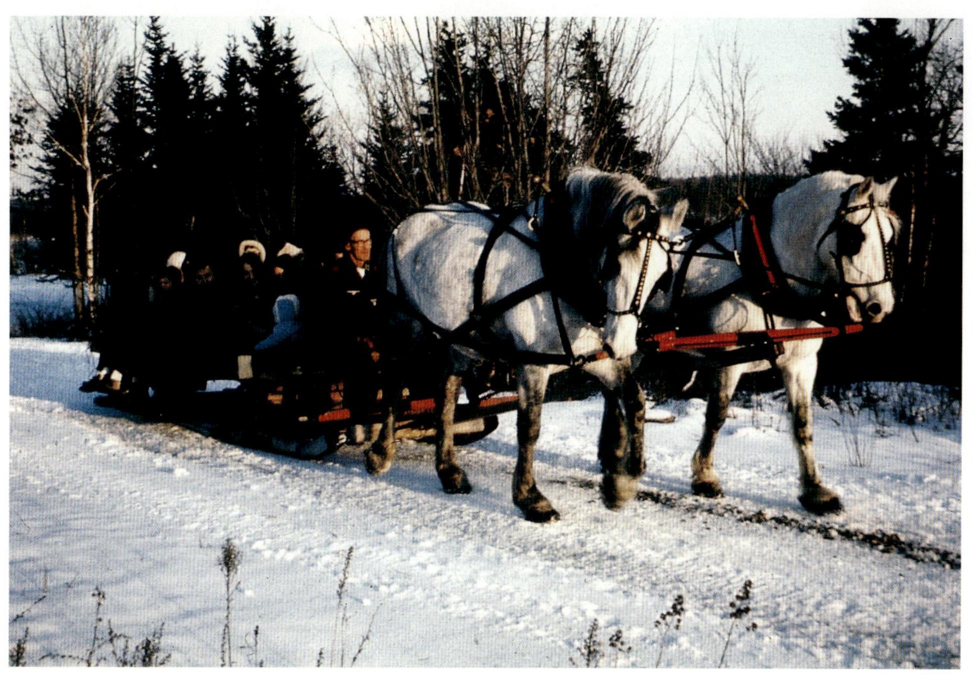

Tain't like someone else. You can't go out all night with your friends. She can't get around like she used to. She can cook some. She does all right what she can do. I don't expect much of her.

Everett Lewis, CBC *Telescope*, 1965

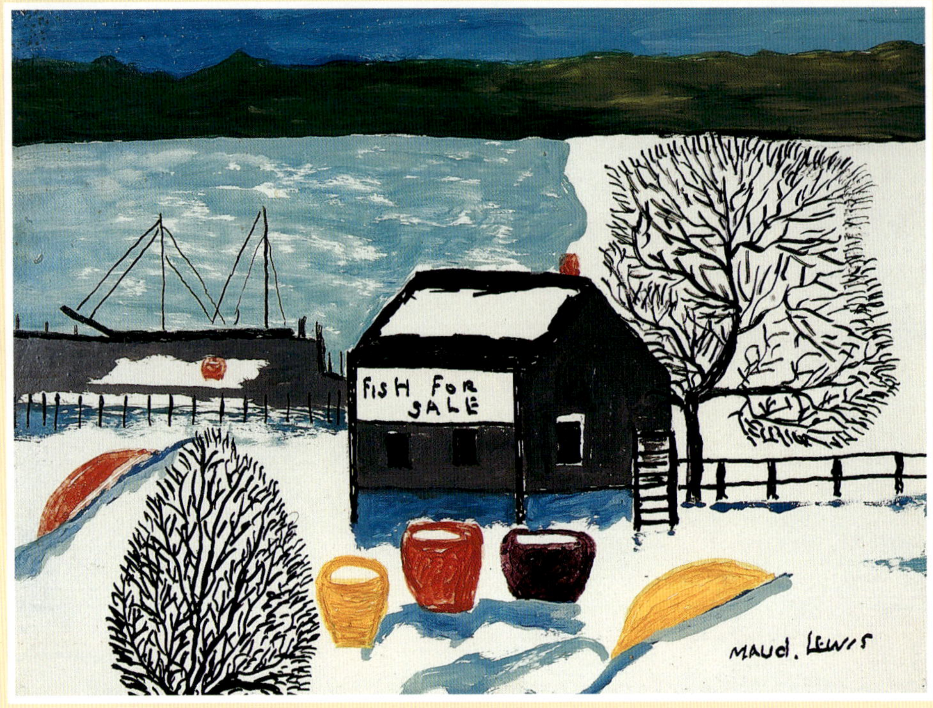

If you are embarking on some type of enterprise to put in words what those pictures are like, you're on a futile enterprise because what happens with Maud is—and it's the same with whoever has this streak of I'll go so far as to say genius … And for me it's a sort of a zigzag streak of lightning.

Phillip Woolaver, Interview, Bear River, NS, 1997

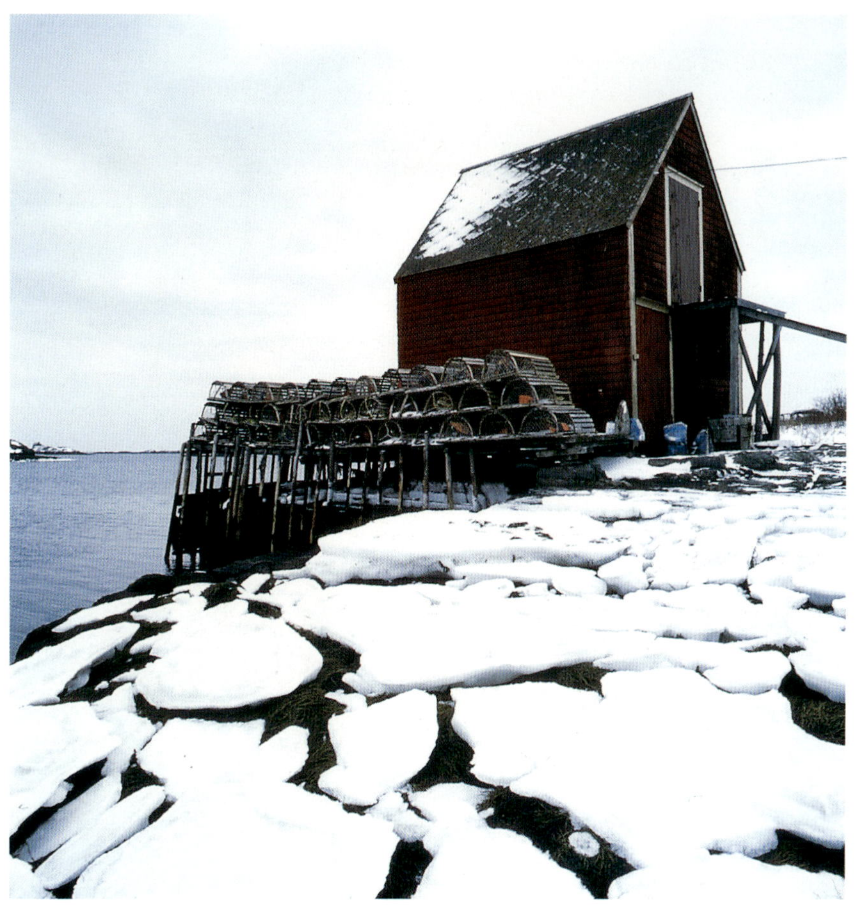

If she was out walking, she would see on Water Street the boats and trains and so on. She would have seen the woolen mill in operation ... she would have seen two lobster factories ... if it was a winter day and she was out, she would have had to wait until the snow plough went by—the horse-drawn snow plough to plough the roads out.

Nate Bain, Yarmouth, NS, Interview, 1997

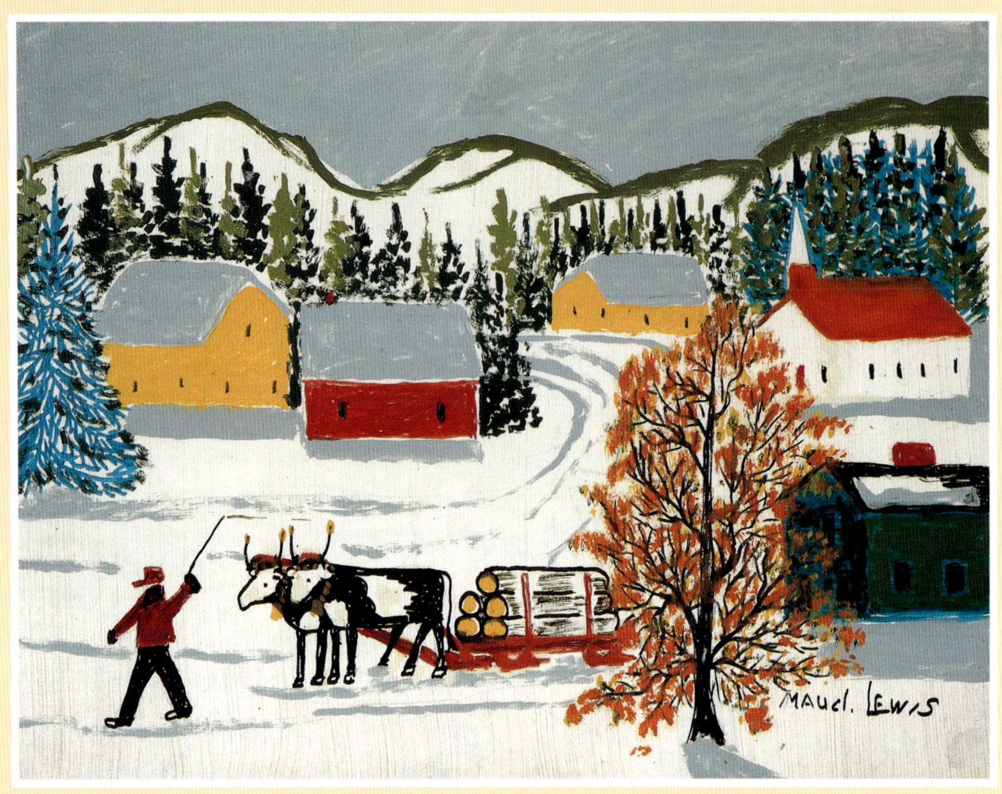

She paints vivid winter scenes—a team of oxen hauling logs,
or perhaps a deer frightened into action.

Doris McCoy, *Atlantic Advocate*, January 1967

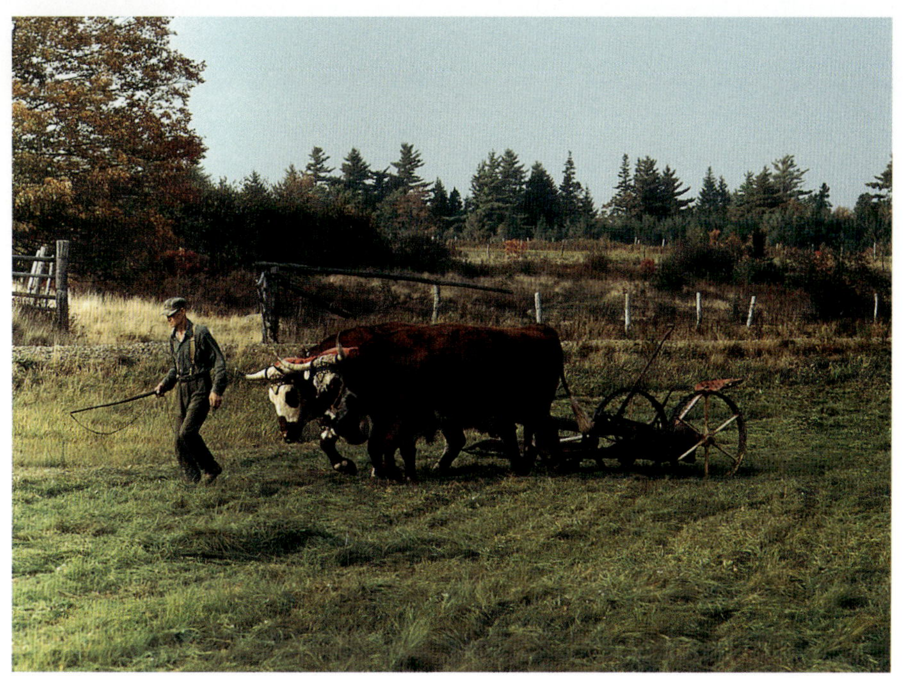

*I got part ways through Grade One. When I went to school they
made fun of me. I was only on the ABC book. I told the woman I
was working for they teased me. I got the prize, writing on a slate.
One cent. Didn't they cry! I bought me a big stick of candy. Went
out to work when I was ten years old. Five cows to milk, night and
morning. All kids had to work then. No pension in them days.*

Everett Lewis, CBC *Telescope*, 1965

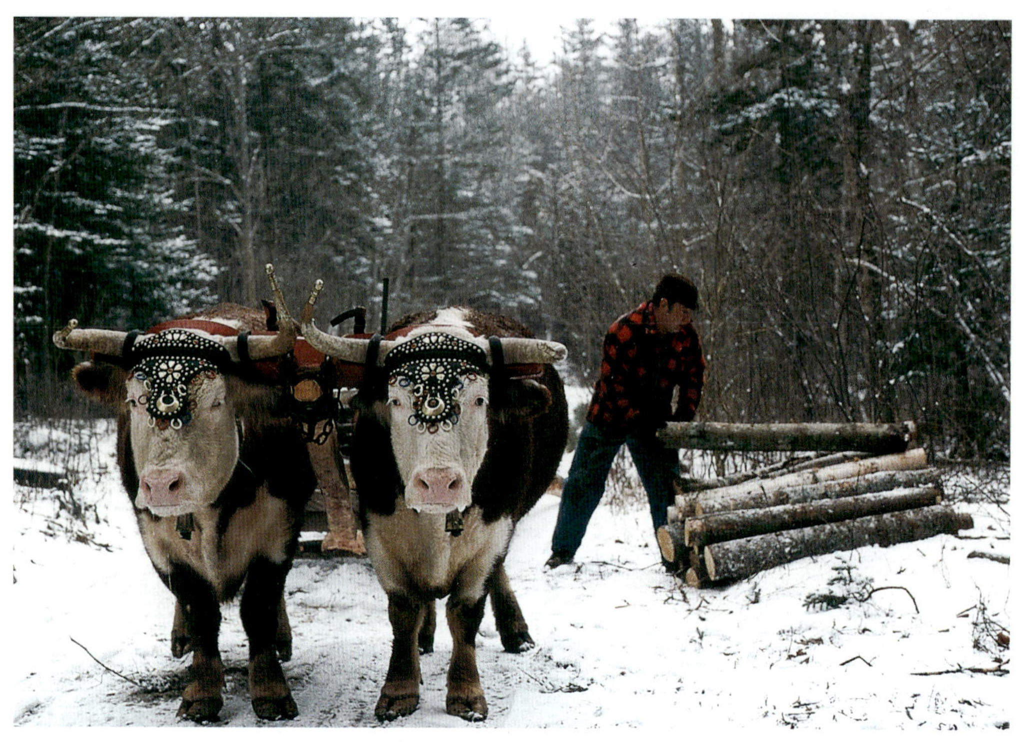

Everett stayed with our family and worked on a little farm we had,
like cutting wood, looking after the animals and things like that.
My dad owned three or four mills at the time and Everett wanted
dad to buy a pair of oxen and let him go in the woods and
haul some of the trees out to the mill. So he did that
for two or three years.

Hugh Dickie, Interview, Digby, NS, 1997

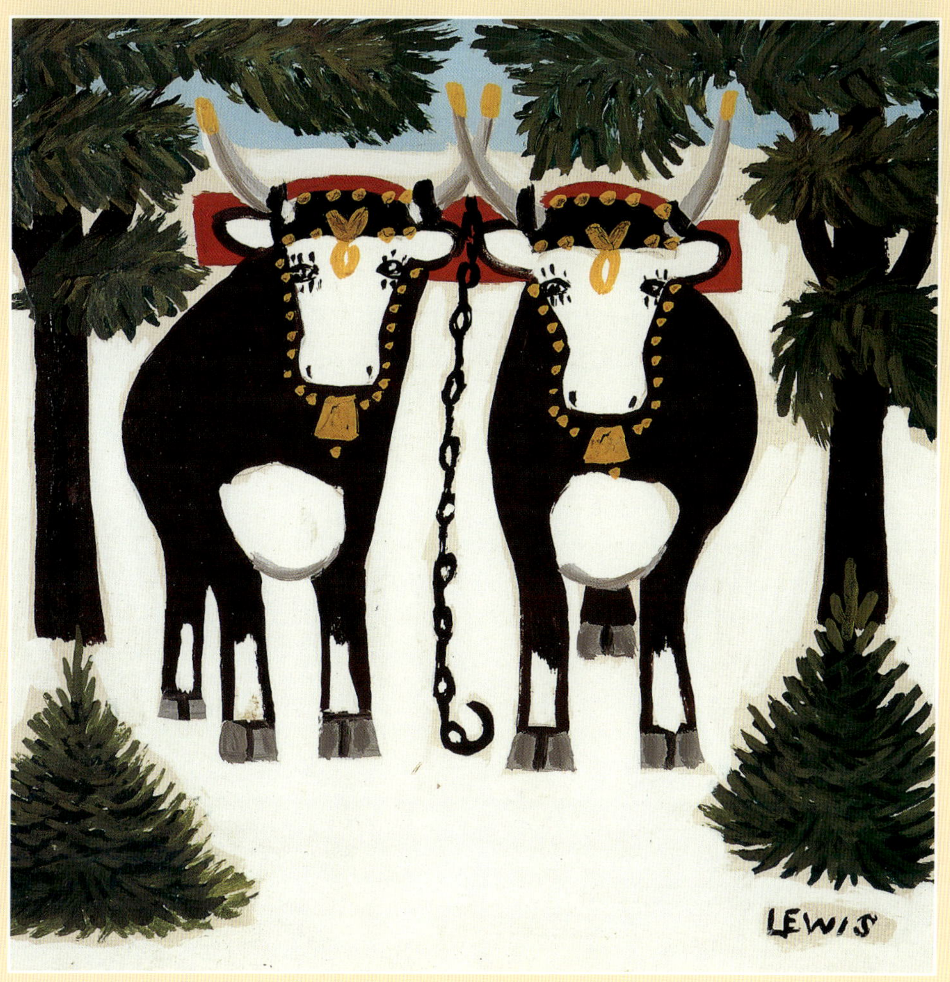

I put the same things in, I never change. Same colours and same designs. I don't copy much, I guess my work up. I don't go nowheres. I put the eyelashes on them to make them look more like oxen.

Maud Lewis, CBC *Telescope,* 1965

Epilogue

*A few years ago I gave the royalties from my play
World Without Shadows to the restoration of
Maud's house. The author's royalties from this book
go to a scholarship for a student in the arts
from Digby.*

—L.W.